Help! My teacher hates me

Help! My teacher hates me

Meg F. Schneider
Consulting Editor: Dennis Meade, Ph.D.

**Illustrations by
David Goldin**

Workman Publishing, New York

Library of Congress Cataloging-in-Publication Data
Schneider, Meg F.
Help! My teacher hates me: how to survive poor grades,
a friend who cheats off you, oral reports, and more. / by Meg
F. Schneider.
p.   cm.
Includes index.
ISBN 1-56305-492-2
1. School children—United States— Juvenile literature.
2. Junior high schools—United States—Juvenile literature.
[1. Schools. 2. Conduct of life.] I. Title.
LA219.S36 1994   94-1093
371.8'1—dc20   CIP
                                                              AC

Cover and book design: Flamur Tonuzi
Cover and book illustrations: David Goldin

Workman books are available at a special discount when pur-
chased in bulk for special premiums and sales promotions as
well as for fund-raising or educational use. Special editions or
book excerpts can also be created to specification. For details,
contact the Special Sales Director at the address below.

Workman Publishing Company, Inc.
708 Broadway
New York, NY 10003

Manufactured in the United States of America

First printing December 1994
10 9 8 7 6 5 4 3 2 1

To my sons, Adam and Jason

Acknowledgments

Many educators and students made
significant contributions to this book.
I thank them all, but would like to single out
a few who withstood the most interruptions during
their busy days to answer my endless questions.
Special thanks to Ellen O'Brien-Scully,
Linda Casper, Lisa Rosenberg, and Joan Snell
for their helpfulness and expertise.
And of course, most of all,
Dr. Dennis Meade, for his sound direction,
keen insights, and absolute willingness to examine
so many issues from so many angles.

Contents

Introduction:

School, with you at the controls 1

Chapter 1: Teacher tension 7

Afraid to ask 11

Favorite teacher leaving 14

Teacher's pet 17

Not working to "potential" 21

Teacher dislikes you 24

Humiliated in class 29

Careless teacher 31

Crush on teacher 34

Too-friendly teacher 36

**Chapter 2: Friendly and unfriendly
mishaps** 41

An average student 44

Teased about a tutor 47

Separated from friends 49

Low on money 51

Rejected by friends 54

Your friend is running for
prez, too 58

No luck with girls .61

Friend joins wild crowd 64

Feeling awkward 68

Self-conscious in the locker room 70

Seeing your ex 73

Uncomfortable with your friends 75

Chapter 3: The great cheating dilemma
. 79

Friend asks to copy off your test 82

Caught cheating 86

Wrongfully accused 90

Plagiarized unknowingly 93

"Changing" your report card 96

Chapter 4: Grade grief 99

Unfair grade 102

The slow class 105

In an advanced class 107

Difficult test 111

Essay writing 113

Nervous test-taker 116

Handling great grades 121

Chapter 5: Homework hang-ups 123

Help at home 126

Undone homework 128

Oral reports 133

Lazy project partner 136

Getting along 139

Late with assignments 143

Chapter 6: Family attention 147

Parents vs. friends 151

Report card jitters 156

Parental expectations 159

Successful sibling 161

Problems at home 167

Chapter 7: Sports spots 175

Endless drills 178

A bench warmer .181

Team pressure 184

Great expectations 187

Slipping grades 189

You're nonathletic 194

Chapter 8: Extracurricular crises . . .199

Nonmacho interests 202

Keeping your own i.d. 207

Job jealousy 209

Losing the lead 213

You're too bossy .217

No time for friends 219

Ready to quit 222

Chapter 9: Physical fears 225

On the school bus 229

Hassled in the hallway 231

Running for help 234

Reporting others 237

Witnessing an attack 239

Frightened of AIDS 241

Drinking problems 245

Chapter 10: Who can help? 249

Afterword: The payback 263

Index 265

School, with you at the controls

If you're like most kids, you have very mixed feelings about school. It's little wonder. A lot is going on. It's where you spend key hours of your day. It's where you make friends, compete in sports, explore outside interests, find romance, and just plain grow and change.

It can be great fun. But that's hardly the whole picture.

School can be interesting but also boring. It can leave you feeling popular or lonely. Some days might seem like a party, others like pure torture. You can be flying high one moment and taking a nosedive the next, wondering exactly why it was you bothered to get up in the morning.

All sorts of confusing, disheartening, and even painful situations can happen. Each can throw you into a quandary, making it seem as if you have no control over anything.

Well, forget that thought, because you do.

Help! My Teacher Hates Me is your guide to taking control of the school experience. It will help you get through those moments when you just don't know how to handle an unfair test, or fear striking out when the bases are loaded, or fight with a friend who wants to cheat off your paper, or have to cope with a teacher you're sure doesn't like you, or encounter all sorts of other difficult situations. You have lots of textbooks on lots of subjects, but you haven't had a book on surviving the pitfalls of being in school.

That is, until now.

How this book will help

This book is composed of situations. What does that mean? Here's an example.

A number of people have finally convinced you to run for class president. You're very excited over your decision, and promptly call up one of your closest friends to tell her so. "Oh, no..." she sighs. "We can't both do it! I'm running, too!"

Each situation is followed by a detailed look at what you can do to resolve the problem. It will include:

◆ an important glimpse into what the other people in the situation may be feeling (you can't resolve a conflict without understanding the position of others!);
◆ actions you might take;
◆ verbal responses you might give;
◆ and a look at the consequences of the different choices you might make.

Sometimes you will find a side box next to a particular situation. This will highlight common variations on the problem you are reading about and how to handle that specific issue. For instance, if the situation is one in which a friend has just asked if she can copy off your test paper, and you really

resent the request, a side box might begin, "My friend needs to copy my homework. I guess it's okay . . ." These are related problems but may involve different responses.

All situations are separated into chapters that reflect the most common areas in which kids experience problems. For easy reference you can refer to the table of contents for the basic situations, but just so you have an idea of what's ahead, here's a look at the coming chapters and the kind of issues they will explore:

Teacher Tension: You fear your teacher doesn't like you; your teacher is perfectly dreadful; you have a crush on him or her.

Friendly and Unfriendly Mishaps: Your friends always want to know your grades; you feel self-conscious in the locker room; the whole class seems to have turned against you.

The Great Cheating Dilemma: A good friend wants to copy off your test; you're accused of cheating when you didn't; you plagiarized unintentionally.

Grade Grief: You believe you were graded unfairly; you panic over tests; you were asked to go into a slower class.

Homework Hang-ups: You didn't do your assignment; you despise your project partner; you can't stand a public speaking assignment.

Family Attention: Your parents dislike your friends; your parents compare you to a successful sibling; your parents expect you to achieve perfect grades.

Sports Spots: Your demanding coach is taking all the fun out of the game; you're having trouble balancing sports and academics; the bases are loaded and it feels like the whole game is resting on you.

Extracurricular Crises: Your outside interests are out

of the mainstream; you're competing with a friend for the lead in the school play; you want to drop an activity.

Physical Fears: Trouble is about to break out on the school bus; you see a student being cornered in the hall; you're afraid of AIDS.

And, a final chapter . . .

The aim of this book is to give you some control over those tricky moments at school that might otherwise leave you feeling helpless and confused. But throughout this book there is a very important and consistent message. Sometimes, despite your best efforts, you will not be able to handle a problem completely on your own.

"When You Need to Talk to Someone" is devoted to explaining the roles of the different professionals at your school. These are the teachers, principals, social workers, school counselors, and psychologists. What they do, how

they do it, and what you can expect from a meeting with each of these people will be fully described.

You may simply need to talk with one of the above people alone, in order to get a new perspective and some important advice. Or you may need intervention, meaning one of these professionals would talk with the person(s) with whom you are having the problem. Perhaps a psychologist needs to speak to your teacher so that your feelings get the attention they deserve. Perhaps a group of kids need to be confronted by a counselor in order to get them off your case.

The point is, it's important to feel as if you can help yourself. But it's equally important to realize you can ask for the help you need.

Adapting advice

It would be nice if school could be a wonderful experience every day. But expecting that it will be is unrealistic, and worrying that there's something wrong with you because things go afoul is equally unreasonable.

You're a person with all sorts of strengths, weaknesses, sensitivities, dreams, aspirations, and expectations. So are all the other students at your school. In fact, the same goes for your teachers.

This being the case, there are bound to be disappointments, confusions, misunderstandings, and tensions. That's what happens when lots of people come together with different ideas. It's a natural part of school life.

So the next time something difficult happens at school, don't crawl in a hole. Pick up this book and try to find either the exact situation or one that is closely related.

Read the advice over carefully and consider how you could use it to your best advantage. If a verbal response is involved, there's no need to use the exact words suggested here. Feel free to bring your own particular personality to the moment. If there is an action required, remember that timing is important. Talking to a teacher "as soon as possible" may not work for you if you can see she's particularly swamped that day.

Just do your best to face the issue, act constructively (keeping in mind the guidelines suggested here), and then move on. Put the problem behind you as soon as possible. Good things are ahead.

Yes, school is a bit like being on a roller coaster. But *Help! My Teacher Hates Me* will help you hang in there for the ride!

1

Teacher tension

It would be terrific if all of your teachers were perfect. Ideally you'd want someone smart, interesting, and funny, a great explainer, a fair grader, an easy tester, and of course, a person who both admires and approves of everything you do. It's a nice dream.

Sometimes you will end up with a teacher who comes pretty close to what you would like. However, for the most part, the person seated at the front of the classroom will be someone with a host of pluses and minuses.

Kind of like you.

He may describe an historical battle with color and flair, but at exam time hand you an essay question that feels like an attack from the rear! She may clarify math concepts perfectly, but deduct major points on a homework paper for the slightest of errors.

Also, occasionally you may be assigned a teacher with whom you just don't click. He doesn't appreciate your humor, and you think he's a bore. It can be a major drag getting along with a person you just don't like. But you will have to cope.

This chapter is about how to navigate your way through a year with any teacher(s), no matter how good or bad, just or unjust, exciting or boring they are. After all, no teacher is consistently anything all year.

And neither are you.

Your goal should be to roll with whatever comes your way in as constructive a manner as possible. And that includes recognizing how you might be contributing to some of the difficulties that arise, and revamping your act accordingly.

The key ingredient to all of this is respect. It's important to remember that you don't have to like a person to respect him or her. Likewise, you don't have to be fully appreci-

ated to receive respect yourself.

It is your responsibility to show respect and to fulfill your responsibility to learn. It is your teacher's responsibility to command respect and to fulfill his or her responsibility to teach. Neither of you is entitled to hurt the other in any way, whether it be through words or misconduct. While it is true you are not equal in power in the classroom, you are both still entitled to each other's respect as human beings. Demonstrating that respect should see you through even the most troublesome year.

Still, at times it can seem as if your teacher is only there to judge you. As if you are powerless against him. As if you are at the mercy of her moods and actions. But these are feelings, not fact. Teachers are definitely there to assess your work. And yes, they set the rules. But you can question them. You can find ways to make your needs heard. And while it's true that a

 teacher's mood may result in an upsetting experience, you can recognize what is happening, take productive steps toward improving things, and seek help if you need it.

Throughout your life, you will have many more relationships that present you with many of the same problems. Other teachers, future employers, forceful friends, and sometimes even close relatives will ask you to recognize your own faults and tolerate theirs, challenge you to improve, and present you with situations that require you to stand up for what you believe in. You might as well start learning right now how to make the most of these relationships.

This includes learning how to be a little charitable!

Teachers are people, too. They have weaknesses and strengths just like everyone else. They have good days and bad days, irritable mornings and endlessly patient afternoons. Besides, you've only got *her* to deal with (which, granted, could be quite a task). She, on the other hand, has an entire classroom of students, several of whom may be driving her nuts!

Occasional tension between you and your teacher is bound to happen. Try and take it in stride. Learning to deal with these complications is an important part of the school experience. You won't receive grades for it, but the skills you develop will serve you well forever.

Afraid to ask

Q You are two days into a new chapter of your algebra text and already you feel very confused. You are dying to ask a few questions. You look tentatively around the classroom. Everyone else looks so relaxed. So confident. So filled with understanding. There is no way you can raise your hand. What if your teacher thinks you're stupid? What if your classmates think you're stupid? Even worse, what if they're right?

A Big news! This is something you should know up front. Right now. Without delay. Any teacher will say that if you put the names and grades of students who ask questions in one column, and the names and grades of students who do not in another, the average grade of the question-asking students is *way* above the average grade of those who remain silent.

So much for your teacher concluding you're stupid.

As for your classmates, consider this: Not everything is how it seems. People who live in big, fancy houses may have lots of money problems. Girls who act as if they think they are beautiful may some-

HELP!

Help! My teacher looks so annoyed when I ask questions!

She may be tired. She may have a lot of material to get through. She may think your question is unnecessary. (Have you been paying attention?) Just listen carefully to her answers. Try nodding when she's through and saying "Thanks." Then, save any other questions for another time, or for a moment when she invites them. If she's not in the mood to be stopped, why push? You can always get to her later after class.

times fear they are very unattractive. And students who nod and take notes as if they "get" everything may be just as confused and anxious as you. Actually, students who are truly confused, or lost or way behind, often don't even know what questions to ask!

In truth, when you ask a question it probably helps lots of fellow students who were too afraid to do the same. The teacher's answer will clear up their uncertainty, and your courage might even inspire them to ask their own questions!

As for resisting the urge to ask a question because you fear it might reveal your stupidity, it is much like a five-year-old ignoring his new two-wheeler because he's afraid he can't ride it. He'll never learn unless he puts some effort into the experience. He *can* do it. He just has to work at it. And so do you.

The fact is, some classroom material is complicated. Most teachers do their best to go through the lessons as carefully as they can. But they also have a responsibility to cover a certain amount of material throughout the year. Therefore, they must keep moving forward. They will not always know if you understand the material as they are teaching it, unless they specifically call on you, for instance, to work out a problem on the blackboard. They are well aware that at least some students could probably use some help. But unless you stop her and ask, she won't know where the problems are and will continue moving through the material.

In other words, asking questions actually helps teachers do their job better. It also inspires them. Teachers who see their students are really listening feel very appreciated. This in turn creates an atmosphere in the classroom of people working hard and well together, and thus learning intensifies in a very meaningful way.

Still, beyond all this is one very important issue. What really matters is not what your teacher or classmates think of your question. What really counts is taking responsibility for your own education.

Only you know what you understand and what you don't. Sure, your teacher will find out eventually through tests and papers, but why wait until then to reveal your bewilderment? Only you can take the action necessary to move productively ahead in your studies. If you don't understand something, say so. Otherwise no one will know until it's too late.

You can't erase a failing grade by going in after the fact and wailing, "But I didn't understand!" In fact, the only thing it will do is elicit the following from your teacher: "Why didn't you say so?"

And that is one question for which there is really no good answer.

Favorite teacher leaving

Q Your favorite teacher has just announced she has to leave in the middle of the school year. You are overwhelmed with feelings of anger and sadness, not to mention fear. You've never done so well in school in your whole life. She inspires you. She makes you feel smart. You can talk to her about so many things. Now what are you going to do?

A First you are going to allow yourself to feel sad. Saying good-bye to someone who has meant a lot to you is bound to be difficult, even if it's not permanent. You have to just go through the feelings. You also have to recognize a fact of life: Time brings changes, and some of these changes may hurt. Friends move, pets get lost, a favorite toy suddenly disappears. A little piece of these changes will stay with you always. And when a difficult change occurs, even if it's only temporary, it may bring up all of those old feelings, suddenly overwhelming you with unexpected sadness.

Try and keep this in mind. It may not lessen the pain, but it will make it more understandable and so perhaps a little less overwhelming.

Anger over a loss is very natural, too. Why couldn't a teacher you hate take a leave of absence, you might ask? Why this one? In fact, why you? This has been your first good year! Well, life isn't fair. It's a fact that makes *everyone* angry. But there's no point letting your anger stand in the way of your accepting and making the best of a disappointing situation. Besides, keep in mind one simple fact. You and this teacher were always going to part ways. When the year was up, she would go on to her next class and so would you. And this is

good. It's important for you to have different educational experiences with different people. That way you learn how to get along with others, how to adapt your behavior to suit different situations, and how to cope with the necessary changes that happen in life. Sure, your teacher's departure is too soon, too sudden. But perhaps your anger will lessen if you consider you were going to have to say good-bye sometime anyway.

And finally, there are those feelings of fear. Here you've done so well, started to feel so smart, and *pow!*—it feels as if someone has taken away your most important ally, and now you're going to have to make do with whatever teacher they send your way. What if that other teacher doesn't see what's special about you? What if he or she doesn't even like you?

What if, indeed. Consider this. Your most important ally is not your teacher. It's you. And the most important thing she gave you is yours now, and that's the sense of your own possibilities. She didn't make you smart. She just made you realize how able you are! If you truly believe she was the best thing that ever happened to you, then realize she is not completely gone. In a way you can carry her with you. You can hear her voice complimenting you or urging you to improve. You can remind yourself of the way in which she attacked a problem and try and do the same. And you can remember the success you achieved in her class and believe in your own capacity to keep it up.

In short, you can be the person you were with her, the you you liked, whether or not she is still your teacher. Chances

are if you feel good about yourself, you will get on just fine with the new person, even if he or she is not everything you might have hoped for. (Actually, you can bet the new teacher won't be. No one can measure up to a person we idolize! In fact, chances are the teacher you adore might have begun, in time, to look a bit less fabulous, too!)

A final note. If the teacher who is leaving is someone in whom you confided many personal problems, there is nothing wrong with asking if you might write her sometime, just to stay in touch. She will probably be more than happy to exchange notes. After all, chances are she'll miss you, too!

Teacher's pet

Q "Yes, Jamie," your teacher says with a big smile as she calls on you for the third time this period. You look around the room self-consciously. Many other hands are raised. People are annoyed and staring at you angrily. You look away in confusion. "Teacher's pet," someone hisses from behind.

A Teachers, no matter how hard they try, will favor some students. Most try to hide it, but they're not always successful. It can be a terrible drag. Still, the truth is, whether or not you're a teacher's pet is not the real problem. It's how you got there that's the most important issue for you. Once you have the honest answer to this question, your options will be clear.

It is quite possible that you and your teacher have similar interests and so he can't help but feel something special for you. Perhaps he's your natural-science teacher and you've both discovered a mutual love of birds. Perhaps she's your geometry teacher and she can sense your excitement over dimension and form. Or perhaps your teacher enjoys your sense of humor and your willingness to make intelligent guesses when a question is asked. Face it! You might just be fun to teach. That's not a crime!

It's your good fortune, and it's your chance to shine. You won't be able to do this in every class. Not every teacher will share your interests or respond to you so positively. Even your friends know that.

So the next time you are accused of being a teacher's pet, when you know you've done nothing more to inspire attention than simply be yourself, stand your ground. "Look," you can say. "Cut it out. I act the same way in this class as I do in others and it doesn't happen there! Give me a break. I'm just doing what I do." Don't accuse your friends of being jealous and don't pretend what they're saying isn't true. They will only end up feeling very defensive, or very annoyed. Be honest. Let them know that, sure, she seems to like you a lot. But be firm, too. Insist you are doing nothing more to inspire this seeming favoritism than honestly enjoying the class. You're certainly not going to stop doing that just for them! Your classmates will pause at that thought. The truth is, you're probably right!

However, what if you have to admit that you are playing up to the teacher? It's not that you like the class so much. It's that you want her to like you, and so you are doing whatever you can to win her attention. And in some ways it seems to be working.

Well, you aren't the first student to feel the need to get on your teacher's good side, and you won't be the last. And actually there's nothing wrong with paying attention to the rules of the class, listening well, and participating with enthusiasm in order to be a well-liked student. It just doesn't work if you're doing it all for the teacher rather than yourself. Because once that happens you usually will step over the line into what some people call "buttering up" or "brown-nosing" the teacher. This is annoying to witness and exhausting to do, even if the results do seem good.

The truth is, a student who feels he has to just keep doing anything he can to please the teacher is usually a student who does not feel confident about whatever he has to offer. It's as if he feels that just being himself, just learning in his own way, is not enough. Only by asking additional questions, doing extra work, and faking interest can

HELP!

My teacher likes my best friend more than me!

Maybe he does, maybe he doesn't. You might want to sit back and observe a few things. Does your friend ask thoughtful questions? Is his work very neat and well done? Maybe you haven't been working as hard as you should. Or maybe your teacher *does* like your friend better. Big deal! Sure, it isn't great. It may even be hurtful. But really, chances are you like other teachers better than him! It's called being human. Anyway, you don't have to be number one on every teacher's hit parade to do well. You just have to work, which is a good thing, because it's a lot easier than winning popularity contests!

he get the approval he craves. Of course, it doesn't really work. Because a person who doesn't feel good about himself and who always feels that he has to do something to make someone like him has a never-ending, tiring task.

The student who likes himself can just be. He works, of course, but his efforts spring from who he is, not from what he's trying to be. He knows his limitations. He accepts his own style. The student who wants only to be what someone else wants him to be must struggle constantly with the question "What should I do now?" And there's always something. Because the possibilities are limitless.

If you are a student who anxiously tries to please the teacher, do understand that other students looking on will feel as if you are trying to get ahead of them unfairly. They are being themselves and getting by, so why can't you? Also, don't kid yourself! Not all teachers respond well to students who try to please

them. You might be getting by in this class, but another teacher might be quite annoyed. Try and tone down your behavior and instead concentrate on simply getting your work done and fitting into the rhythm of the class.

Certainly it's important to meet your teacher's expectations, but it's equally important to respect your own interests and personality. It might be a good idea for you to see a school counselor or psychologist, or to speak to your parents. You might need some help in learning to appreciate all the special and particular qualities that you naturally possess. Many people need to learn that who they are is more than good enough, and you might be one of them.

Being called a teacher's pet is never fun. Being on the receiving end of name-calling never is. But people who call others names are usually those who feel insecure about themselves. Your classmates want to do well and feel liked, too, and are perhaps envious of your success. If you're doing well in class on your own enthusiastic steam, then just smile and say, "I like this class. The teacher knows it. So sue me. But if in truth you have been buttering up the teacher, just nod, say something like, "Okay, okay," try and cut back, and get some help . . . for your sake more than theirs.

Not working to "potential"

Q You are having a conference with your teacher about your work. He is in the process of reviewing your English paper when he suddenly looks up at you and says, "I don't think you are working up to your potential." You're confused. You *are* doing your best. Maybe you just don't have the potential he thinks you have—whatever that means.

A Before getting into how you might handle this disheartening and, for some, embarrassing situation, let's consider the more important issue. Exactly what does the word *potential* mean?

Potential is a very subjective term. You can't measure it and you can't prove it. You can only believe it exists based on the things you can measure and can prove. A person's potential to be or do something is an assumption, though it may indeed turn out to be a fact.

But here's the thing. Not all potential is realized. You may have potential that you simply can't or won't use. Perhaps you could be a wonderful pianist. The talent is definitely there. But you just don't have the personality to practice for hours every day. You might indeed have the potential to be a terrific foreign-language student, but perhaps this is a year in which science has grabbed your interest. It turns you on. Something about learning languages is leaving you bored and frustrated.

When someone tells you that you have the potential to do something, he is saying it appears, from other things he knows of you, that you ought to do well. But he is not taking into account your problems, your personality, your interests, and where you are at this point in your life. All of these

things affect your potential . . . or rather, affect your performance.

So let's get back to the situation at hand.

Your teacher has just told you that you're not working up to your potential. He's telling you that he thinks you can do better.

First, realize your teacher is actually complimenting you, whether or not he's right about your potential. Because the truth is, he came to his feeling by noting all of your many strengths. The fact that he isn't allowing for the possibility that you are doing the best you can, based on who you are at that time, is something he needs to think about carefully.

And there's something you need to think about carefully, too. Striving to reach your "potential" may be a foggy, elusive goal. But striving to do the best you can is not. In fact, it's the most important thing you can do for yourself.

So, before you write your

teacher off, carefully consider whether he has a point. Ask him exactly what aspect of your work seems to be weaker than it should.

Were there many misspellings? Was your paper not carefully planned? Were your ideas not presented in the most organized way possible? Then, listen to his answer. Perhaps you'll agree, but perhaps you won't. It may be that your potential is not equal to your teacher's expectation or simply isn't in gear right now. At this time in your academic career, paper writing is not your strength. Perhaps you will find that strength soon. Or perhaps you won't ever find it there, but you will enjoy it in other subjects.

As noted in the teacher's pet discussion in this chapter, teachers want to see their students do well. It makes them feel good. If they see a student who shows every sign of being bright and able, they want to see that student shine. It means they've done their job well. It means they're good teachers.

But it also means they may occasionally place an unfair burden on their students. Try and understand that this is not intentional. It is born of their understandable need to feel successful.

The next time a teacher says you're not living up to your potential, ask him to explain why he believes that to be so. Then, if you think you are doing the best you can do, *say so.*

"I'm really trying. This was the best I could do, but I'll keep at it."

And be proud. It's not easy to be the best that you can be. And it's a drag to feel as if that's not enough. Sure, no matter what, you should keep trying to improve. But only to feel yourself grow and learn. Not to prove your supposed potential.

Teacher dislikes you

Q It's time to enter your classroom, but you find yourself making up excuses not to go in. The fact is, you don't think your teacher likes you. She picks on you. She grades you harshly, and even the softest whisper to a neighbor causes her to whirl around and give you the evil eye. It's a miserable feeling.

A No one enjoys being around a person who doesn't like him or her. It is very unpleasant. Depending on the power this person has, it can also be scary and infuriating.

Still, the first thing you should do when this sensation hits is a reality test. We all have moments of confidence and moments of insecurity. How we feel often affects how we "read" things that are going on around us. Before you do anything, it's important to know if what you are feeling is really based on fact or on your own very personal fears and worries.

If you have other teachers, consider how you feel when you're around them. If you fear they don't like you either, chances are you have a tendency to feel rejected. This is something you should talk over with someone who can help you, such as a parent, school counselor, psychologist, or trusted teacher.

If in fact this is the only teacher with whom you have problems, next time you are in class, notice how she behaves toward other students. Does your teacher snap at them as well? Ask your friends how they feel in her class. It's possible you are very caught up with your own hurt feelings and are failing to see that her manner in general happens to be quite brusque and short-tempered.

If it appears that she is being rough on you, consider as honestly as you can your own behavior. Ask your friends to be frank with you. Do you talk a bit too much out of turn? When you do speak out in class, is your tone unpleasant, or sarcastic, or terribly tense? Teachers are social

creatures just like you! They won't respond very well to someone whose behavior sets them on edge.

Obviously, if your friends report you do act improperly, see what you can do about changing your behavior. But if this doesn't help, or if your friends claim your behavior doesn't seem to be out of line and they have noticed this teacher is rough on you, consider this . . . It happens. It isn't fair. It isn't nice. You have every right to be angry about the situation. But life is like that. You will, over the course of time, brush up against many people who do not respond well to you. It will feel bad. You will hope you can turn things around. Sometimes you'll be able to, sometimes you won't. Mostly you will simply have to learn to work with the situation. In school, depending on which grade you're in, this might entail several different strategies.

If she is your teacher

throughout most of the day, your situation is more difficult because you can't quite get away from it. You can elect to do one of two things. First, you might decide to take extra care with your behavior and work, in an effort to make it through the year with as little conflict as possible. Second, you might ask your parents or a school counselor to intervene. This will likely become necessary if you do put in that extra effort and are still being treated with hostility.

Sometimes a parent/teacher conversation will clarify what is really going on. Perhaps your teacher is unaware of her behavior. Perhaps you are doing something annoying in class of which you and your friends are unaware.

Unfortunately, there is a risk to bringing in a third party. You might create a situation in which the teacher feels very defensive, and then you end up feeling as if you've made a bad situation worse. See the note on page 28 for some specific suggestions your parents might employ when talking to your teacher.

If you are in a higher grade and the teacher instructs you only in history or geometry or English, you might want to take a laid-back approach. Since you presumably get on well with your other teachers, you could simply concentrate on completing the course and moving on next year to a more comfortable situation.

There is, however, one exception. If the dynamics between you and this teacher deteriorate to the point that you are receiving unfair grades, it is extremely important that, with the evidence in hand, you speak to a counselor, a trusted teacher, and certainly your parents. Sometimes a teacher will allow his or her feelings to interfere with the grading process. He or she may not be aware or want to admit that this is happening, but it doesn't matter. You have a right to stick up for yourself. School records should be a reflection of the quality of your work, not of personal conflicts.

Finally, it might be easier for you to handle this difficult situation if you understand why it happens. Sometimes we love people who remind us of people we have loved. Sometimes we take a disliking to people who remind us of someone who brought us pain. Other times we have good or bad feelings for someone depending on the kind of event with which they seem associated in our mind. We may also react badly to people simply because they have personalities that seem to clash with our

HELP!

My teacher always accuses me of whispering in class, but it's not me he's hearing!

So tell him! But do it privately and calmly. Indignantly crying out "That wasn't me!" once a day won't help. You need to get your teacher alone. You need to look him in the eye so that he can see your sincerity. If you go to that much trouble, chances are he'll assume you're telling the truth.

If your teacher then asks you to identify the person who was talking, simply say you really don't know. She may not believe you. And in fact, you may be telling an untruth. But it's an unfair question in the first place. You shouldn't be asked to get someone else in trouble.

own. Certainly you can think of people who, for no particular reason you can readily identify, get on your nerves!

Perhaps your teacher is responding to something in you that reminds her of someone else, or some other experience, or some painful moment. It's not your fault. It's not anything about you. Unfortunately, however, it is your problem.

Your teacher should be able to control her reactions. And you have every right to be angry that she hasn't. But try to remember this problem will end. Concentrate on the people who do adore you, and complete your work.

That's the best way of as-suring a smooth transition from a teacher who doesn't like you to one who really does!

Note: In order to increase the odds of a positive conversation, parents might do well to comment, "My daughter (or son) has been having some trouble in your class. She seems unhappy. How do you feel she's doing?" Walking in and throwing out the line "My child thinks you hate her" will only cause your teacher to defend herself instead of looking at the problem. As much as possible, the teacher should be brought into solving the problem and not be made to feel as if she is entirely responsible for it.

Humiliated in class

Q Your teacher is giving back the class papers. Arriving at yours, she holds it up and announces, "This looks like a first grader's work. It's sloppily written and the spelling is very careless. Adam," she adds, turning in your direction, "I expect better things from you."

A First of all, there is no justification for publicly humiliating anyone. If your teacher has something critical to say to you or anyone, then she should always say it in private.

The most important question you have to honestly ask yourself is "Even though she shouldn't have embarrassed me like this, did I leave the door open?" In other words, did you give the teacher cause to be so clearly frustrated by your performance? Did you create a situation in which she could become disappointed and angry? Certainly you wouldn't expect or want her to respond the way she did, but is it possible that you handed her a paper that said, by its quality, "I don't care about my work"?

When you hand in a sloppy paper, talk rudely, or whisper during class, you have to remember you're taking a chance. You're breaking a very important rule: You must respect the school experience. This can get many teachers very upset, and rightfully so. Since no one is completely predictable, you never know what might happen. Your teacher could reprimand you quietly one day, and be forthrightly angry the next. She could smile patiently one time, but snap quite fiercely another.

If you are publicly humiliated by your teacher under circumstances you might have avoided, go ahead and be angry. But take some responsibility, too.

However, if your teacher has humiliated you in a situation where you could not have changed your behavior, then you are in a very depressing situation. If she says, "I had your brother in my class two years ago, and *he* was such a strong student. What's the matter with you?" while everyone is listening, you are likely to want to fall in a hole.

Listen to her quietly, and when the class is over, go off someplace and have a good cry, or punch a punching bag or beanbag chair or go run a mile. Talk to a friend or counselor if you need to. And then decide what you want to do. You might elect to approach your teacher the next day and explain that you are doing your best and that it hurts to be compared to your brother. Or you might decide to let it go, put in some extra effort, and hope she doesn't do this again.

Of course, if this pattern continues you may have to

seek intervention from a third person, though it is unlikely that a teacher would continually put down a student in such a dramatic manner.

But most important, no matter who did what to whom, keep this in mind: While you might remember the humiliation in colorful, horrible detail for weeks, it will soon fade for other people. They're too concerned with their own problems!

Careless teacher

Q It is the third time this month your teacher has failed to catch all the mistakes on your spelling test. In fact, just last week he started a science experiment and then forgot to complete it. You and your classmates had to remind him, but by then it was too late. He pretended it didn't matter. But it did—to you. You are beginning to feel angry, and cheated out of having a teacher who really cares.

A It's no wonder you feel distressed. School can be a tough and challenging place to which you are supposed to bring the best you have to give. If you have a teacher who is not pulling for and with you, the whole experience can feel like a bad joke.

Still, the first thing to do is clearly assess in your mind the time frame of the problem. Everyone is entitled to have a bad day, or even a bad week or

two. But, a teacher who, for an extended period of time, is not doing his best to inspire a class, or who is not concentrating on his job, needs to be confronted with the problem.

The most important thing to realize about a situation like this is that you are the consumer. You are the person who had to stand up and say, "I am not getting what I deserve." And the people you need to say this to are your parents.

You need to bring them precise examples both from your experience as well as from those of other classmates. You might encourage your parents to call the parents of your friends to gather evidence that this is not a problem just between you and your teacher. Still, in order to give the teacher the benefit of the doubt, and also perhaps to inspire him to focus once more, your parents might conference with this teacher "to see how

Kathy is doing." They might comment lightly that you feel as if the class wanders a bit, and see what the teacher has to say. If he claims to have no idea what they mean, and if nothing then changes, it's time for another strategy. A few parents might elect to speak to the principal about the problem.

Hopefully the principal and the teacher will then be able to resolve the situation. A teacher may have become ill, or overwhelmed with a family problem, or simply feel tired from the years of energy he had put into teaching. As a result, his performance in the classroom may be suffering. Whatever the issue, it is something the teacher must face.

At this point you might start to feel guilty or a little anxious that you've caused such an uproar. After all, your teacher seems to be all there, sometimes. Well, the truth is, sometimes isn't good enough. Sure you can and should have compassion for whatever his problems might be. But there is an unspoken agreement between a teacher and a student that must be respected. Teachers are obligated to teach, and children are obligated to learn. Students cannot learn if teachers don't do their job. It is your responsibility to speak up if this, unfortunately, is happening in your class.

It doesn't make the teacher a bad person. And it doesn't make you a tattletale. It makes all of you people with a problem that has to be sorted out in order for you to get what you deserve.

Is a good education worth getting a teacher "in trouble?" Well, don't think of it as in trouble. Think of it as informed.

And you bet it is.

HELP!

My teacher was told to shape up, but he didn't! Why don't they just fire him?

Teachers have contracts that protect their positions. If the teacher isn't willing to go, it can be a long, drawn-out affair until he is finally out of the classroom. Since it appears no one is watching, it might be tempting to get lazy and not work. Bad idea. All the other classes of your grade will continue moving ahead and next year you may find yourself way behind. If you're stuck with a poor teacher, you can form a study group with your friends and manage on your own. Or, if it's a critical class or he's your teacher in many subjects, you might talk to your parents about tutoring. Your teacher won't mind. Actually, if he's that bad, he won't even notice!

Crush on teacher

Q You have a secret that is really embarrassing. You can't stop thinking about your teacher. You think he's handsome, smart, funny, and very sexy. You haven't told anyone because you feel very silly. Still, you can't help wondering what would happen if you shared your feelings with him . . .

A The first thing you should know is that crushes on teachers are very *normal*. They're not bad, or forbidden, or silly. In fact, it would be somewhat unusual if you got through your entire school experience without having a crush on one or more teachers.

After all, think of the dynamic between the two of you. Your teacher is up there in front of you looking in control and sounding very wise. He is, in a way, performing for you—working to keep your interest. If he is particularly successful at gaining everyone's attention, or at any rate yours, it must be because he does indeed radiate something quite exciting. So, as you stare at him day after day, which is unavoidable, it's easy to start fantasizing. "I bet he's fun to have dinner with," you might think, Or, "Boy, he must be fun to be with on a ski

34

slope." Of course, you don't know if any of your dreams about him are true. (He may be very different in his personal life than he is in the classroom.) But as you sit in your class, watching him day after day, your assumptions about him may seem like fact.

Being attracted to a teacher, dreaming about him, or wanting to be with him outside of school are all normal feelings. The trouble only comes if these feelings are so intense that they begin to affect the way you function academically or socially. If your grades begin to slip because you can't concentrate, if you aren't interested in other guys, or if you shy away from opportunities to be with your friends because all you want to do is dream, then your crush may indicate you have more than just that.

What you may have is a problem that is very important to face. Sometimes a crush on an authority figure could mean that you feel a need to lean on someone, to be protected, or that you are wrestling with

problems so big that kids your age just seem inadequate to handle them well.

If you are overwhelmed by your feelings for a teacher it would be a good idea to speak to a school counselor about the problem. Don't be afraid or embarrassed. Developing a crush is a very natural and common attempt on the part of many students to resolve difficult personal issues. As you talk to someone who is there to listen, you will probably discover that something else much bigger than your feelings for this teacher is actually bothering you. Once you begin facing the real problem, your feelings for this teacher will probably lessen.

But whatever you do, try to resist the temptation to tell your teacher how you feel either in words or in deeds. First of all, if he is as professional as he should be, he will politely but firmly put you off. This is bound to be terribly upsetting and embarrassing to you. The truth is, it is just not appropriate for any student to be too familiar with his or her teacher. There is the age difference, of course. But there is also the simple fact that your teacher is there to teach, not to form personal relationships with the students.

And the same is true for you. You are there to learn, not to become emotionally involved with your teacher! And should something like this de-velop, your teacher could lose his job and your work would undoubtedly be affected. It would be a very unhealthy mess.

This separation between student and teacher is critical to the healthy atmosphere of the classroom. No one, not you or your teacher, is supposed to cross the line that divides you.

Too-friendly teacher

Q Your new teacher is acting in a way that makes you uncomfortable. You can't quite tell if he's kidding, but he seems *too* friendly. Some of the remarks he makes about the way you look embarrass you, and the other day you couldn't help feeling that he was standing a little too close. You actually took a step backward to get away!

You must tell some-one. It doesn't matter if you're not sure, or if you think you're being immature, or if you are worried you're overreacting. If you're uncomfortable, you need to discuss your feelings with a trusted adult. This could be your parents, another teacher, or a school counselor. This is so for a very important reason.

You need to understand what is going on, and you need support in doing so. What follows applies to the above situation and to any other kind of related incident.

Before you get too distressed, you need to assess a number of things. Is this a pattern, or just an isolated incident? Certainly, if the comment has upset you, you should seek help from another adult. But do be clear about whether or not it has happened before. Your parent or counselor will help you assess whether or not this is something over which you need to stay concerned.

Next you will want to consider if this is a teacher who just doesn't realize he's making you uncomfortable. Perhaps he's just one of those people who doesn't see why girls and/or women feel uncomfortable or unhappy when a man who is not supposed to be looking at them in a male/female way does. Describe the teacher's actions to someone and the situation you were in when the incident occurred. This person may be able to help you assess if the teacher merely needs to be told that comments like this make you feel bad, or if something more ominous is going on. In other words, is this a person who simply needs an education in what is known as *sexual harassment?*

Before we go any further, it's important to point out that sexual harassment is not just a male teacher, female student thing. It happens between female teachers and male students. It happens between female teachers and female students. And it happens between male teachers and male students. It's distressing no matter what form it takes because it's abusive behavior.

You might have heard a lot of talk in the news about sexual harassment in the office. This is when men who are supposed to be looking at women as coworkers make it clear they look at them as something more. Sometimes it's just a comment or two, sometimes it's out-and-out body contact. Women find it upsetting, and sometimes even frightening. The men who simply make a comment or two sometimes don't understand this. They think it's "harmless."

Well it isn't harmless, because if it were harmless, women wouldn't be upset. Right?

These men in the workplace need this explained to them, and so does your teacher.

If you can't tell your teacher how you feel, you

HELP!

Everyone thinks my teacher is gay. He and I get along real well. I'm worried that means he's going to be attracted to me.

It doesn't. He probably likes you, though, and that's great. Gay people (if he is gay) are too often treated as if they have no ability to choose appropriate partners at appropriate times. Sometimes people think if a man is gay, then he's going to feel attracted to all males. But that's no more true than the idea that you would be attracted to every female! P.S.: Just because you like him doesn't mean you're gay, either.

might suggest that a school counselor do so without mentioning your name. You might also look to see if he does it to any other girls, and if so, perhaps you can all go in together and speak to the counselor. Talking about this kind of issue can be very difficult. There's nothing wrong with getting support from friends. After all, you did nothing wrong.

The situation becomes even more serious if your teacher makes any physical advances toward you. This would include anything from just touching you on your shoulder a bit too often or seductively to actually making a more obviously sexual move, such as touching a private part of your body, or attempting to get you alone through physical pressure (pulling you into an empty room, or verbal threats, "you should be nice to me, if you want good grades"). You must report this immediately. It is a very serious problem and potentially a dangerous one to both your physical and emotional health.

Unfortunately, many girls who experience this problem keep their mouths shut. They feel guilty, somehow fearing they did something to bring this trouble on. "I did try to look pretty today," they might think. "Maybe I asked for it." Well, that simply isn't so. Looking pretty is your right. It's not an invitation. Also, many girls feel scared that if they report the teacher they will get into trouble with that teacher and all other authority figures in the school.

In fact, not telling anyone about this problem is the most dangerous thing of all. Grown women often find it hard to cope with physical advances from men with whom they work. As a result, they say nothing and suffer terribly. Their work may go downhill, and so might their self-confidence. They start feeling depressed and angry a lot of the time. Imagine how much more difficult it must be for you to cope! Not to mention the fact that if you don't report the problem, chances are this teacher will go on to upset other students as well. Someone has to stop this damaging behavior.

Now a word about making a mistake. As stated earlier, any action, any word, any physical move on the part of your teacher toward you that feels too personal *is* too personal. In other words, you have a right to your feelings, and to draw the line where you see fit. However, consider two things. One, you might have been in a particularly sensitive mood one day, and while your teacher should perhaps not have commented on how pretty your hair looked, it does not necessarily mean there is something dangerous brewing. Your sense of personal boundaries might be shifting as you mature. It might be difficult for even

you to know how you feel from one day to the next about a particular interaction. Two, your teacher may have a professional lapse. Of course, he shouldn't, but since he is a human being, one comment, meant in a harmless way, may slip that perhaps should not have.

The bottom line? If you don't like what a teacher says, respect the feeling. And under no circumstances should a teacher touch you inappropriately. You'll know when that is. If he grabs your arm in congratulations, you will likely feel just fine. If he touches it in a more personal way, you won't. Trust your instincts and get some help. Don't wait. Don't give yourself time to worry about getting into trouble, or whether or not you are to blame. You're not. You're the child. He's the adult.

And you deserve better.

Chapter **2**

Friendly and unfriendly mishaps

Chances are you and most of your very closest friends attend the same school. Most of the time this probably feels just fine. You share similar experiences. You enjoy the good times together and muddle through the bad. You always know the others are there.

But you must have noticed that it's not all bliss. You don't always get along. Friends get hurt. Angry. Confused. Sometimes you might even fantasize about switching schools and leaving all those "great" friends behind!

This is no surprise.

First, there is the simple fact that constant togetherness can create conflict, misunderstandings, and confusion.

Second, no matter how close you and your best friends might be, you are all separate people with very different needs. One friend might be sensitive and quiet, another more aggressive or demanding. One might have a very weak ego and need constant assurances, while another might be rather conceited, making her difficult at times to be around. Also, during the school years you and your friends are constantly changing and growing. What you need and expect from each other may be in constant flux. You may hurt a friend as you explore a new style of behavior, or you may be hurt by a friend who is experimenting with new relationships.

Third and finally, while you may all travel in the same social world, the people in the other parts of your lives are different. Parents and siblings, to name only a few, will all exert differing sorts of pressures upon each of you. Family problems, sibling rivalries, and even such issues as money and health can disrupt a friendship with lightning speed.

As a result of all these differences, each friend might expect or demand many special things for you, just as you might expect and demand particular things of them.

The trouble is that it's very difficult to be everything for everybody. Thus, friendships sometimes experience rough spots.

This is when attending the same school can really make for tough situations. You can't get away from the people you are hurting, and you can't hide from the people who are really hurting you. All of you have to exist together in the same classroom, gym, auditorium, or lunchroom. Add to this the everyday pressures of school itself, and you can see why friendships can sometimes shudder under the strain.

But that's okay. That's life.

Good solid friendships offer an opportunity to learn how to resolve conflicts, see that anger doesn't blow caring away, and understand that all of us, in the end, need each other, especially when there are problems.

Also, and very important,

school life is an opportunity to learn how to balance friendship with other responsibilities. This is a skill that will serve you well throughout your life.

Real friendship is not a conflict-free relationship. Rather, it's a relationship that can weather conflicts and still remain warm, trusting, and fun.

So the next time you start dreaming about switching schools, consider this. People, or rather friendships, are the same no matter where you go. And so are you. Running away solves nothing. It only offers temporary relief. You'll learn a lot more about yourself, your friends and life if you stand your ground, and work out your problems.

Otherwise you'll simply take them with you. Only they'll have different names and faces.

An average student

Q The grade on your history paper is not what you were hoping for and you feel very disappointed. You're an average student and it sometimes embarrasses you that you're not better. The moment you walk out of the classroom, your friends begin comparing grades. "Hey," they call out, "What did you get?"

It's important for you to recognize two things.

One, your grades are absolutely your own business. It is your right to keep them to yourself, and it is your right to share them. But they are *yours*, plain and simple.

Two, grades are not a reflection of you as a person or, necessarily, your intelligence. They are, however, a reflection on how well you are learning, or your test taking, or writing skills, or any other capacity being judged by the grade.

Certainly poor grades are a problem, and we will get into that in other parts of this book. But poor grades, in the situation above, can feel especially embarrassing. You might feel ashamed in front of your friends, or even afraid. You might worry that they'll conclude you're dumb. Or that you can't keep up with them. You might be afraid of their pity or, worst of all, rejection.

HELP!

Everyone aced a test but me!
I feel like crawling in a hole!

That happens sometimes. Maybe you studied the wrong material. Maybe you misunderstood one basic piece of information and it affected every single answer. Maybe you just weren't concentrating. Whatever, it doesn't have to be a sign of things to come! Just tell any friend who asks how you did, "Not great. I must have been asleep," and then do your best, either on your own or with your teacher, to figure out what went wrong. Then forget about it. It's time to move on, build up your confidence, and work toward a better grade next time.

But try to remember, no good friendship is based on grades or academic standing in class. Grades don't have a sense of humor. They can't comfort an unhappy friend or entertain at the lunch table. They don't say just the right thing when a buddy needs some confidence building, and they certainly can't offer caring advice to a confused friend.

You can bet that if your friendships are based on grades, then those are only passing friendships. (Excuse the pun!)

Still, the problem remains: What do you do when asked about your grades? You certainly don't want to offend your friends, or make them feel as if they're rude or selfish for asking. Sure, chances are they want to compare their grades to yours. And yes, they might feel relieved if you haven't done much better, and even great if they've done the best of all. But it doesn't mean they want you to do poorly. Therefore, your response should be as matter-of-fact as you can make it. The style of response you choose will depend on the way in which you usually relate to your friends.

You could smile mischievously and say, "I won't ask you yours if you don't ask me mine." If your friend insists on blurting his grade out, you might then say, "Well, good for you. I'm keeping mine to myself. Nothing personal. Believe me."

Another, less flip response might be, "I didn't do as well as I had wanted. This is not my best subject. I'll get it together, but in the meantime, do me a favor. Don't ask."

Either response should shut your friends up pretty quickly. Certainly they will assume your grade was not good, but so what? The overall impression you will leave them with is that you are a strong person, with a balanced view of himself, who can't be pushed around. That's the kind of person people love to be friends with.

Teased about a tutor

Q You have been going to an algebra tutor for a few weeks. You've kept it quiet because you're afraid that people will think you're dumb. But your secret's been discovered, and now several of your friends are teasing you.

A The truth is, despite what it might sound like, your friends are not worried about whether or not you're dumb. They are probably, however, concerned about one of two things (if not both). One, they may have a need to feel "smarter than" you. Teasing is a good way to feel stronger and bigger and smarter. Of course, they don't realize it's also a sign of insecurity. Two, they might be very worried that since you are getting help, you will actually top their grades. Heaven forbid!

But there's something else, too. If you were hiding a tutor,

47

what makes you think one (or more) of your friends isn't nervously hiding one as well? Not to mention the fact that many students receive tutoring of a more informal nature at home. Perhaps an older brother or sister is helping. Maybe someone has a mathematician for a mother. You never know. Not that you should worry about it. What matters is you.

How do you respond then when some friends begin to tease you about tutoring? The fastest way to shut them up is to behave as if it is the best decision you've ever made. This should be easy, since it probably is.

"It's the smartest thing I've ever done," you could say proudly. "It's making my life a lot easier." If someone asks what you mean, you might say, "I get the work done more quickly. It's great. I understand everything. I'm lucky."

What can your friends say to that? Probably nothing.

The truth is, tutoring has gotten a bad name. Perhaps this is so because years and years ago there were fewer tutors, and only students who were flunking out considered hiring them. But these days a tremendous number of students with passing grades visit a tutor for one subject or another. Seniors are constantly being employed to help younger students strengthen their academic skills.

Finally, by answering your friends directly and with pride you will be doing yourself—and more important, them—a very big favor. Chances are one of them will go home that night, stumble over a difficult school assignment, and consider, without fear or embarrassment, the possibility of seeking help.

That should make you feel pretty good.

Separated from friends

Q You and your three closest friends were in the same homeroom last year. It was great. You studied together, you complained together, and you shared special times together. But now you've just gotten your class assignment for the new year, and this time only you are in a different class. You're nervous that you'll lose your friends.

A Very young children usually make friends based on toys they enjoy, games they like to play, or whether or not they are neighbors. Older children, however, choose friends for more significant reasons. Can they trust each other? Do they make each other laugh? Are they comforting to each other? Do they make an effort to be sensitive to each other's feelings? These qualities are not inspired by being in the same homeroom.

They are, however, qualities that can be sorely missed.

It's easy to fear that you'll be out of the loop. You may

fear that your friends will stay buddy-buddy and that somehow you will get lost in the shuffle. You may think you won't have as much in common and as a result there will be less to talk about.

Well, there is no point denying the facts. There will be some things you won't have in common. You won't be able to complain about the same teacher. Your tests may be a bit different, your homework harder or easier, and your surrounding neighbors, a different set of faces. But this does not mean you'll run out of things to say.

The essential *you* will stay the same. Your personality will not change. Your ability to be sensitive and caring and trustworthy will remain intact. And don't underestimate the year of togetherness the three of you have already shared. That can never be taken away.

In other words, all of the things that worked together to build your friendships will still be there. You simply won't be physically together as often.

And actually, you should count yourself lucky for that. It's a funny thing about close friendships. While they can be wonderfully supportive and warm, they can also sometimes box you in. You might miss out on making other friendships. This in turn can make you very dependent on your little circle, which definitely has its drawbacks. What happens if you get into an argument? Will you be brave and stand up for yourself, or will you cave in because these are your only friends? The best friendships are those in which people are there because they genuinely care— not because they have nowhere else to turn.

If you get separated from your friends, it's natural to feel a little envious and a little insecure. But keep in mind that there are clear advantages. They are bound to miss you, you will have an opportunity to form new relationships, and while you may not have the exact same experiences to discuss, your news will be that much more interesting. You, in other words, will bring something fresh to the mix.

Getting separated from friends is a chance to remind yourself that you can do okay on your own. Having close friends you can depend on is a lovely thing. Feeling that you cannot depend on yourself is not.

Low on money

Q Most of the kids you hang out with wear very hip clothes. The trouble is, the clothes cost money and your family is on a tight budget. Even the extra money you earn has to go for everyday expenses like lunch. You feel terribly uncomfortable about your limited wardrobe in front of your friends, and also fiercely jealous.

A There is no doubt about it. There will always be people who have more than you, no matter who you are, and there will also always be people who have less. Some will have had a hand in what they possess, others not. It's not a fair system. But it's life, and we have to live with it.

Given that, it's very important to look at the part of this problem that you *can* change. Certainly, yearning for things you don't have is a disheartening experience.

But chances are it's not just the clothes that are bothering you, or even the big houses or fancy bikes, which may also be causing you grief. It's probably more your desire to fit in.

Many people, young and old, no matter what they can afford to buy for themselves, have that desire. And just about all of them, no matter what they have bought, *still* worry about it.

Somehow "fitting in" rarely comes easily.

There is a reason for this. We can only be who we are. We can never be just like someone else or some other group, because what makes us individuals will always get in the way. The trick is to feel se-

---

HELP!

Everyone thinks the new girl in school is weird. I like her, but I think my friends will think I'm weird, too, if I hang out with her.

You've got to get brave. You can't run your life according to what other people think. If you do, you won't be making decisions that feel good. They'll just feel safe. Safe decisions (like ignoring this girl) will ultimately bring boredom and frustration. Follow your own mind! If your friends say, "Why are you spending time with her? She's so strange," just say something like, "So what if she's a little different? If you knew her, you'd see some really great stuff." Be firm. Say it like you mean it. Chances are some of your friends will believe you. It's that "attitude" thing again.

---

cure enough about who we are that when we differ from the crowd, we use our energy to embrace that difference instead of shoving it away.

Of course, there is something else we can do with our energy, and that is to make ourselves feel more comfortable in whatever way is available to us. In your case, if clothing is the concern, then you might try and create a look that is similar to the more expensive version but which you can afford. In doing so, you might put a very special "spin" on your style, one that others could come to admire and perhaps even envy.

It all depends on your attitude.

People who dress the same way look at each other with some relief. "Aha," they are thinking. "I'm okay." Others, sensing this attitude, buy into it. They think, "Gee, that person seems to feel okay, so he must be." Now, what if you looked a little different? What

if you added something hip to your look that you could afford? And what if you walked around with the attitude, "I'm very cool?"

Lots of people would buy into that, too.

No one is going to like you just because you dress like they do. And no one—except very insecure people who need to see themselves reflected in everyone else—is going to reject you because you don't. You may confuse a few people. Others might wonder exactly who you think are, and keep a little distance for a while. But keep this in mind: If there's one thing that people very much admire, whether they show it or not, it's a person who confidently and intelligently does his or her own thing.

Perhaps this is because it gives all those people who are trying to fit in a little hope—the sense that if they were ever ready to just be themselves, someone out there might think that's actually just fine.

Rejected by friends

Q Suddenly you're the class outcast. You don't exactly know how it happened. One day you seemed to be getting along with everyone just fine, and the next a small disagreement led to a full-scale rejection. You can barely bring yourself to go into the lunchroom.

A There are several things for you to consider here.

First and foremost, keep in mind that full-scale rejections rarely stick. Some if not most of your former friends and classmates will come back.

When an entire group of people have decided to turn their backs, they are usually just following each other. Their hearts aren't in it. It's not you; it's the power of the crowd that is egging them on. As soon as one or two people change their minds, others will follow and you'll be back "in" again.

Second, no one likes admitting to mistakes. And certainly people can be cruel. But still, if this kind of mass exodus takes place, there is a chance that you have been behaving poorly to one or more of your friends. Perhaps resentment had been stirring in many people and when one got really boiled, they all just followed. If this is true, you might need to offer an apology. It needn't be a big production. Simply walk over to a person whom you've cared about and wronged somehow and say something like, "I think I've been a little selfish lately. I know you're mad at me, and I'm sorry." Don't grovel. Don't repeat it a hundred times. Your friends may not accept you back with open arms that second, but chances are you'll drift back together in short order.

Third, keep in mind that any mistake you might have made has probably gotten

blown way out of proportion. That's what happens when people start talking. You might have told someone, "Jane was real moody on the phone yesterday." The next person repeats your comment to another friend, saying, "Lisa thinks Jane is very moody." That person then passes the thought along to someone else, saying, "Lisa only likes people when they're happy. She's dumping Jane, you know." The only thing you can do under these circumstances is to track it back. Find out who said what to whom, and when you figure out where the confusion started, speak up! Clarify the situation as quickly as you can. When people are "living" together in such close proximity, rumors fly. Your best protection against them is you!

However, it is quite common, unfortunately, for a group of kids to gang up on someone for no particular reason. It's usually born of insecurity. This kind of "You're bad and we're not" behavior somehow gives this crowd a feeling of power, strength, and superiority. It makes them feel big and special together, which they like because deep down they probably feel shaky and ordinary. The individual members often forget to view themselves as separate from the crowd—as people with their own opinions and strengths.

That is one of the downsides of being in a crowd. On one hand, it can provide you with lots of built-in friends and security because the crowd operates as a unit. On the other hand, while a crowd may "embrace" as a unit, it may also "reject" as one.

Which brings us to the issue of what to do if you've done nothing wrong. While it may seem to you that everyone has turned away, chances are there are some kids who haven't. They just aren't in your crowd. Perhaps it's time to seek them out. Of course, you can't treat them like a booby prize. It isn't fair to view them as second best. If you want to open up the pos-

sibility of friendships with new people, then you should stick with it no matter what happens with the old. If old friends return, it would be rude to drop the new ones, and very unfortunate for you. For one thing, you could be missing out on some terrific friendships, and for another, if and when this kind of mass rejection happens again, you really will be all alone. And you'll deserve it, too!

Finally, do take the time to consider exactly who these people are with whom you've been friends. The fact that they've ganged up on you doesn't make them all bad. There's no point blaming them or hating them en masse. (That's a lesson you've just learned the hard way!) People have weaknesses. Perhaps you can remember a time when you did the same to someone else. But you should be clearer on the individuals in your crowd, and the individual in you. The best friends are the ones who listen to their own minds.

Perhaps you might, when things calm down, try and do things one-on-one with different friends. Really get to know them, and let them know you. Offer your own opinions more often—in a noncritical way, of course. ("I'd rather do something different this afternoon. How about ice-skating?" will work better than "Why do you guys always want to do the same thing?")

By building a more personal and honest connection

HELP!

I just found out my good friend has been saying mean things about me behind my back!

Yes? From whom did you hear this? When did she hear it? What exactly was said? And to whom? Are you sure you know the facts? People exaggerate. People misunderstand. People lie. You must remember this when you hear that someone has said something to someone about you. Then go straight to the source. Tell your friend what you've heard, making it clear you're not attacking her.

"Someone told me that you said . . . It hurt when I heard that, and I found it kind of hard to believe." Then, and only then, will you stand any chance of knowing what really happened. Probably something did. But most times, it won't be quite what you heard. Once you know the truth, try and talk it out face to face—even if it hurts. Otherwise you'll only be inviting more back-biting.

---

with each of your friends, this sort of mass attack is less likely to happen to you again. And it is less likely that you would be drawn into a similar withdrawal from some other person in the future.

Chances are, as you get to know your friends in a more intimate and trusting way, you will discover that each and every one of them has moments in which they want to step away from the crowd. Or simply disagree with it.

And maybe you'll all decide that's okay. The crowd can stay intact. It's just that its borders should be less guarded. You and everyone else can venture out and speak your minds, and yet still be there for each other.

It will make a far happier crowd than the one you've been in.

Your friend is running for prez, too

Q A number of people have finally convinced you to run for class president. You're very excited over your decision, and promptly call up one of your closest friends to tell her so. "Oh, no . . ." she sighs. "We can't both do it! I'm running, too!"

She's wrong. You absolutely can "both do it." You simply have to "do it" carefully, with sensitivity and respect for each other's ambitions, and with constant awareness of your friendship.

You have to make a formal verbal agreement.

The agreement has to cover how you will conduct yourself during the "campaign," and in so doing, it will protect your friendship during this complex time. There are many issues to consider.

♦ Will you discuss the campaign at all?

♦ Will you argue about each other's priorities or qualifications for the job?

♦ Will you publicly speak out negatively about each other's qualifications?

♦ Will you be allowed to talk someone out of voting for your friend?

♦ Will you be allowed to create campaign slogans that make fun of your friend?

♦ During the campaign, will you see each other socially, or

do you think it would be best to put things on hold?

♦ Do you agree, once the campaign is over, to resume your friendship no matter who wins, and no matter what angry issues have surfaced? In other words, do you both agree to understand that this situation could get very stressful, and that once it's over, you both want your friendship back on solid footing?

Consider all of these issues, and any others that might come to mind, as carefully as possible. Talk about them openly. Get out all of your concerns.

And then abide by everything you decide.

No sidesteps. No excuses.

If, during the campaign, you feel the need to change what you've agreed to, talk to your friend about it first. Make sure the understanding has changed and then stick to those new rules. The object here is to give each other as little reason as possible to be distrustful of the other.

You'll note that the agreement does not include behavior the moment the winner is announced. This is so for one important reason both of you need to understand. It's easy to say, "The winner will congratulate the loser and that's that. Then we'll go back to business as usual." But when disappointment hits hard, it isn't easy to go back to anything. Certainly a simple "congratulations" is important, mature, and necessary. But whoever loses may have to lick her wounds. This might include avoiding the winner for a little while in order to gain perspective on the election.

If you win, you have to understand this. But there are things you can do so that your friend will more easily be able to reenter your life. First, you might tell her when she congratulates you that you could really use her help in your new position. Ask her to let you know when she's ready to talk about it. Second, you can then leave her alone for a while.

She's not going to want to hear the world congratulating you. It's not that she wishes you ill, it's that she wished herself to win. If she doesn't bounce back immediately, don't be offended. She's just human. She's just disappointed. She might even be just a little bitter. Probably she fought hard to win. It didn't work. You'd have felt terrible, too.

It's painful when two good friends have to compete against each other for anything. It doesn't matter if it's a part in a play, a track meet, or an election. The issue is the same. You care about each other, but you care more about realizing your own goals. Don't be ashamed of that. It doesn't make you a bad person. It makes you a motivated, self-respecting person—just like your friend, who is undoubtedly feeling the exact same way.

That's why you like each other. People like people who like themselves.

No luck with girls

Q The guys have been teasing you unmercifully. You haven't had any luck with girls yet and everyone knows it. It's gotten to the point that you don't want to run into your buddies in public places for fear of what they'll say.

A No one moving through their preteen or teen years is confident with the opposite sex. In fact, no one in their twenties is either. Actually, to be perfectly accurate about it, no one at any age is completely confi-dent when it comes to ro-mance. The friends who are teasing you are as anxious as everyone else about girls. But by putting you down, they are hoping to feel better about themselves. That's really what teasing is about—feeling big by making others feel small. It's cruel. It's not nice to make fun of anyone, even in jest. Your friends know that as well as you do. But they've got a need that is stronger than what they know: "I need to feel like I'm doing better than other people. I need to feel okay."

Chances are they've chosen you as a mark because you haven't had much obvious luck with girls. You've never had a "girlfriend," and sometimes if you ask a girl to dance, she says no. Perhaps your friends are only doing marginally better, but that doesn't matter. You're a safe target to tease because they know you're a worrier.

There are several things you can do to protect yourself under these circumstances, but first you have to understand the realities of your situation so that you can respond with confidence. Everyone matures at a different rate. Some of your friends

might be more developed physically than you, others more confident and sure-footed. It doesn't mean you won't get there. It just means you'll get there at a later date. Many a popular movie star has told the story of not being able to find a prom date.

Being attractive to the opposite sex is a hot button for everyone. Most of us are afraid we won't be. But you should realize that just because someone is tapping into your worst fear, it isn't necessarily true. You may in fact be attractive to a number of girls who can't quite find a way to let you know, or you may be concentrating on only one girl when you need to spread out a bit. Also, take a long, hard look at those kids who are teasing you. Just exactly how successful are they? The truth is, it's usually the kids who are most anxious about their own attractiveness who tease others.

And finally, understand that this culture puts forth many images of the "successful, smooth male." He's handsome, he's smart, he's cool, and he gets the girls. Well, guess what? He isn't real. Measuring yourself against the images we see on TV is a losing proposition. It's like a child crying because he can't fly like Peter Pan. Sure it would be nice, but human beings just don't do that. What good is crying going to do?

So, what do you do when you're being teased? The object is to shut your friends up as quickly as possible.

If you're feeling reasonably strong and are given to flip remarks, you might respond with something like, "I don't exactly see a long line of girls knocking at *your* door," then laugh and change the subject. This will give the impression that your friends' teases are not going to get you down and you're not opposed to striking back just a little to protect yourself. Chances are they'll shut up from fear of what else you might say. (Remember, your friends probably aren't superconfident, either.)

If, however, you tend to be more serious, you might simply say, "Hey, why are you coming down on me? I'm trying, you know." Usually, if these guys are really your friends, they will just back down. You'll have shamed them into being decent and fair. Sometimes people need that little push.

What you don't want to do is simply say things like "Stop it!" or "That's not true" or "Leave me alone." These are purely defensive answers. They don't inspire anyone to stop and think. They don't inspire anyone to look at you or themselves with honesty and feeling.

Finally, later that day, you might want to call a particularly good friend who was teasing you and say, "Look, don't do that again, all right? It makes me feel bad. I wouldn't do it to you." He may laugh. He may claim you're too sensitive. He may not be able to discuss it with you at all. But he probably will honor your request.

Friend joins wild crowd

Q You're becoming very concerned about a close school friend. He's begun hanging out with a wild group of kids and his grades are slipping. He looks incredibly cocky one minute and miserable the next, and you're even afraid he's experimenting with drugs.

A You will probably want to help him. That's how friends are. Don't think, however, that you possess the cure for his problems. You don't. What you do have is caring. That's a significant gift for anyone who is hurting.

But, this caring has to be transmitted thoughtfully, though. Otherwise it may not be interpreted as caring at all.

It will be heard as criticism, and that is the quickest way for all communications between you and your friend to shut down.

The best way to help your friend is to know, as much as possible, what's going on inside of him. That can only happen if you can engage him in a trusting conversation. This might be very tough. You might feel really nervous and fearful of making your friend angry or of turning him off. Remind yourself that the more important issue is your friend's well-being. Chances are your worst fears will not be realized, especially if you follow these pointers:

♦ Find a good time to talk. Don't catch him by his locker where he might fear others can hear, or in between classes when you know the clock is ticking. Instead, call him during a time when you think he'll be hanging out at home or actually arrange a time and place where the two of you can be alone to talk.

♦ Ask him questions in a way that won't threaten him or make him feel as if you are sitting in judgment upon him. Don't say, "Boy, you've been getting into lots of trouble. What's the matter with you, anyway?" Instead, try, "I heard you got into trouble yesterday. It sounded pretty bad. What was going on?" You see the difference? It's compassion, not criticism.

♦ Make observations that sound more curious than accusatory. Don't say, "Wow, your grades have been slipping like crazy. Those guys you hang out with are really dragging you down." Instead try, "I know you've been having trouble with school lately. Algebra's tough."

♦ Reveal your interest in how he's feeling, but without sounding too intrusive. Don't say, "You've looked really miserable lately. Why haven't you told me what's going on with you?" Rather, try, "I get the feeling you're not too happy these days. Is there anything I can do?"

♦ When you listen, concentrate, and be clear about what he is telling you. Reflect back his words so that you can be sure. "So you're saying that these new guys are fun, but every once in a while you think maybe they're a little dangerous?" This will allow your friend to see you are truly trying to understand. He will take that as a sign of caring. And in turn, you will have a more accurate picture of how your friend feels.

Of course, none of this may immediately inspire your friend to open up, but it will keep communication open between you. Chances are some important thoughts will emerge and at least you will have set up a dynamic between you that is positive and non-threatening. The chances of him asking for help if a crisis really hits will be much higher.

If your friend does reveal some painful things to you, try and be as compassionate as you can. Allow him his feelings. Don't say, "That's silly! You're very smart," or "Don't be ridiculous. Your old friends think you're great." These statements may sound supportive to you, but they are not addressing his feelings. They are, in fact, denying them. Instead try, "I don't think you're dumb at all." Or, "Why do you think your friends don't care about you? It's just

not true." Besides, people who are very upset are often far more upset about things they can't bring themselves to discuss. It's easier to complain about simpler things. Sure, he might feel dumb, but it might be something much more profound that is upsetting him. As much as possible, get him to talk about the feeling. "Look, I want to help. Maybe it would feel good to talk with me about it." Doing so is bound to give him some relief and get the two of you a lot closer to the real problem.

The truth is, you are not likely to get at what's really troubling your friend. If you do, great! But after establishing that you care, and that you're willing to listen to him with an open heart and mind, you should probably suggest that he speak to someone who can help him feel better. Refer to the back of this book for a list of various people he might consult and offer to go with him if it would help him to reach out.

Finally, your friend may

not be open to any real discussion with you. The moment you say anything, no matter how nonjudgmental, he might turn on you or stalk away. Or he might simply tell you to mind your own business. If you think your friend is not in any grave danger—meaning you don't sense he is about to hurt himself in any way—then it's up to you to decide the next step. You might want to walk away, saying something like, "When you're ready to be reasonable, let me know." This would be nice, because chances are he's not happy, and if you're a real friend you'd want him to know you're willing to work it out when he is.

However, if you see him going from bad to worse, or if you feel your friend might be so depressed that he could hurt himself, or that the gang he is hanging out with is in some way endangering his health, then you should let someone in authority know. Again, refer to the list of people at the back of this book.

This is not tattling on a friend. This is helping a friend. You must be clear about this. The problem your friend is having is too big for you to handle on your own, and it's too big for you to keep to yourself. But it is just the right size for you to discuss with a person in a position to help.

And then you are going to have to go about your life. You may feel hurt, sad, scared, worried, disappointed, and even angry. This is a good friend, and he's moved away from you in an upsetting way. But the one thing you will not, or at least should not, feel is guilt. You will have done everything you can.

There is a limit to how much anyone can help a friend. In fact, there is a limit to how much a professional person can help your friend, too. Your friend has to want to help himself. And that is something he has to come to on his own. Lots of people can try and help him get there. But only he can turn himself around.

Feeling awkward

Q You have just entered junior high and are feeling very self-conscious in front of the upperclassmen. Every time you walk by them you feel out of place, as if you just don't really belong in this school at all.

A It is perfectly natural to feel this way. These are new circumstances, you don't know your way around yet, everything seems strange, and on top of all that there is some truth to what you're feeling! You *are* the youngest in the school. You are probably not as mature-looking as the older kids. You know it and they know it.

But here's something else you should know.

Last year, the class ahead of you felt the exact same way. And two years ago, the class ahead of them were also cringing in the hallways. And to be honest, when you hit high school, and then college, and when, as an adult, you walk into the first day of your new job, you're going to feel in some ways just as self-conscious and scared.

It's called being new. It's called not being hip to the system. But most often, it's called growing pains.

Anytime you start a new phase of your life, it's going to feel scary. There are so many unknowns. But once you become more comfortable with what is expected of you, you will relax. Most likely by the time the year is well under way, a lot of your discomfort will have passed.

Sure, you may still have your moments of feeling like one of the "babies" in the school. Sure, upperclassmen may occasionally look down on you. (Probably a lot of

---

H E L P !

My neighbor, who's two years ahead of me, sometimes hangs out at my place on weekends. But at school he completely ignores me!

Everyone wants to be cool. Everyone worries what others think. Lots of people feel it isn't cool to hang out with a younger person. They're afraid people will think they're immature, or that they can't get friends their own age. You probably have some of those feelings, too. So don't push it at school. Let him walk on by. Then make your choice. If you're really bugged by his behavior you can ignore him back, even when you're on your street. If you're not, you might want to give him a break and enjoy his company on the weekends.

those kids feel they've earned the privilege. After all, they were looked down on themselves!) But as the year moves forward you will grow increasingly more at ease in school. It will become *your* school. You'll know the way it sounds, looks, and feels. And as that happens you will feel more and more a part of it. Being aware of your "status" won't be nearly as trouble-some—just, perhaps, a little annoying.

But you can handle that because you know that next year it will all be over! When the new class of students comes in, it will be their turn to feel out of place and *so* young . . . giving you an opportunity to express your sympathy and understanding. (But, of course, only if you feel like it!)

Self-conscious in the locker room

Q You feel extremely self-conscious in the locker room. A group of kids are always commenting on everyone else's body and it makes you feel awful. Your body's okay, but it's not what you'd have liked. At least not yet . . .

Few people are satisfied with their bodies. Even famous fashion models could draw up a list of their own imperfections. Right now you might feel you're not developing fast enough. Later, you might feel you don't like the way your development "turned out." This is a very body-conscious world, and unfortunately most of us are caught up in the issue.

It's important to keep this in mind, not just in terms of feeling more confident about your own body, but in realistically considering the people who do the staring and whispering. Chances are they are as concerned and worried about their own bodies as you are about yours. Their defense against this anxiety is to make you so anxious about your body you won't stop to consider theirs.

A brilliant plan!

But you're onto it now.

Of course, that doesn't make it all that much easier. Knowing why you're self-conscious won't necessarily get rid of the feeling... though it will hopefully take the sting away. Here are some practical pieces of advice that would help in the immediate situation:

♦ At the beginning of the year, if the lockers are arranged in aisles, try and make sure you and your friends take over a line of lockers so that you can stay together and protect each other.
♦ Why not come to school partially dressed for gym? Slip a T-shirt on under a sweatshirt. Wear shorts under sweatpants or baggy jeans. After gym you can slip your clothes back on, and then later you can run into the bathroom and change in a toilet stall when no one is watching.
♦ If you're on close terms with a teacher whose class is right before gym, explain your discomfort in the locker room. Ask if you can sit near the door, and bolt as soon as the bell rings so that you can change before everyone gets there.

♦ If you are required to take a shower, things could get a little difficult. Try to make sure a few good friends are showering next to you, wash up as quickly as possible, and keep a towel close at hand.

♦ If the scene in the locker room is particularly mean-spirited, report this to either the teacher or a counselor at school. Truthfully, but sadly, this is not unusual. Someone will probably be sent to monitor the room so that taunting and teasing is at a minimum.

♦ If someone does slip in a nasty or teasing comment, you might consider striking back. But don't double the wrong by pointing out that person's particular flaw. Simply saying, "I wouldn't talk if I were you . . ." or "So you think your body is so great?" would suffice. Chances are he'll leave you alone after that

and spend an awful lot of time trying to figure out exactly why you think his body may not be so great.

Locker rooms can be nerve-racking places. Physical appearance is a sensitive spot for almost everyone, but especially when everyone is going through changes. Knowing this should help a little. People are complex packages of looks, brains, and personalities, and should be seen as such. Unfortunately, locker rooms direct attention mostly to the looks.

So get out of the locker room as soon as you can! But as you go, take a look at those kids who've been teasing you. Chances are they aren't quite ready to leave just yet—and probably because they want to get everyone out of the locker room before they take their own clothes off!

Seeing your ex

Q You and your girlfriend have split up. You feel heartbroken and would rather not see her again. The trouble is, she's in one of your classes and you have to see her every day. You're so upset each time you see her that your work is beginning to slip.

A Heartbreak can be horribly painful. It can feel so bad that it's as if nothing else in the whole world matters. No one who has ever been in love, or at least in "heavy like," would ever deny this.

But while you have every right to feel the way you do, you have another right also— the right to take care of yourself the best way you can, and to then get on with the rest of your life.

Heartbreak needs time to heal. It's an intense feeling that deserves respect. You cannot sweep it under the rug. You have to go through it. To do so you will probably need help. It's important to talk out your feelings with your friends, older siblings, or parents. No one escapes heartbreak. It's nothing to be ashamed of. If friends and close relatives cannot seem to help, it might mean that you need to talk to someone else, such as a school counselor or psychologist.

You may think this is an

issue they would not take seriously, but that isn't so. Romance and love are a part of life. They can easily affect everything about you, including your schoolwork. If your grades are slipping, it would be a good idea to let a counselor know why. He or she can bring a special, more experienced perspective to the situation that friends and family cannot. He or she might be able to get at the true root of why you are having such trouble getting over the hurt. Sometimes it's not just the breakup that is causing such pain. It can also be that it has stirred up difficult feelings about yourself, or about feeling abandoned in general. Once those feelings are looked at, your pain might subside.

The point is, you need to take care of yourself and your terrible hurt so that you can get on with your life. You might be able to move a few seats over in class, but the school is not going to transfer you to another class, or your ex to another school. It's a tough situation, and you are going to have to come to terms with the breakup so that you can once more focus your energies on your work, your friends, and, yes, a future romance!

It isn't easy to be near someone with whom you once shared a special closeness. This is especially true if you still have strong feelings but the relationship just wasn't working. It's your right to feel sad. It's just not your right to allow those feelings to ruin friendships, muck up your family life, interfere with your hobbies and interests, or drag down the quality of your schoolwork. You owe more to yourself than that. Your heart is broken. Your life does not have to be.

Heartbreak deserves respect, but so does every other aspect of your life.

Uncomfortable with your friends

Q You are hanging out with a crowd now that is starting to make you uneasy. They get a little wild, sometimes they drink, and you're afraid they're only going to get worse. The problem is, you can't seem to get the courage to step away. You want to, but you also feel drawn to the crowd.

A A good way to begin leaving this crowd is by understanding why you haven't yet. There are many reasons why you might not be able to step away. It very much depends on who you are and your own specific problems. But here are a few of the more common reasons:

♦ You might be lonely. You might have been feeling like an outcast at the time that you were drawn into the crowd and you're afraid you'll be alone again once you leave.

♦ Sometimes when people walk on the wild side they are doing it to strike back at people who have hurt them or don't seem to care. It's kind of an attention grabber. It's a way of saying, "Hey, I bet you'll look at me now!"

◆ Living dangerously is also a way of blocking out other painful feelings. It can get so scary or thrilling that those feelings simply overwhelm any deeper hurts you might have.

◆ A part of you may simply be seeking to find a balance in your life between serious responsibilities and cutting loose. Sometimes when people get involved with a crowd they aren't comfortable with they are doing it to experiment—to try and find that place where they do feel comfortable.

The trouble with all of this is that crowds can be very seductive. No matter why you get into it, or how much you might want to get out, a crowd can be a powerful pull. "Come, be like us," the members seem to be saying. "We'll stick by you. We're cool." And for you, at this time, this is very tempting.

But the fact that it's tempting doesn't necessarily mean it's good. Or healthy. Or even fun. It simply means that something is drawing you to it. Something is filling you with a sort of desire.

So the question is, can you satisfy that desire another way? Can you feel less lonely, or get attention by saying you need it, or face what's really hurting you, or discover who the real you is, without this crowd?

Yes. You can. You may not be able to do so on your own, however. There is no shame in that. But it would be a terrible shame to want to leave, not do it, and then find yourself in a bad situation. It's not too late to leave now, it's just hard. There's a big difference, and if you wait too long, you might find out just how big that difference is.

If you can't talk to a friend or family member in a way that helps to give you strength, refer to the back of this book for a list of the various professionals at your school who will be able to help.

Don't expect things to

turn around immediately. Don't expect that you will be able to just say "good-bye" to these friends after one meeting with a teacher, counselor, or psychologist. The issues you are dealing with may run deep. It could take a while to uncover why you have needed this crowd and to find the strength to leave. (Then again, after a session or two with a counselor, you might feel as if you can just walk out!)

Also, the crowd might make it difficult for you to leave. They may hassle you. They may accuse you of being chicken, or immature, or any number of things. As a result you might feel even more con-flicted. You might begin to fear you simply aren't free to do what you want.

But you are, and here's a trick. If you can't just say, "This is what I want to do," then try blaming it on other people. "My parents are really on my case. I've got to chill out or I'm dead meat." You might also try, "The principal actually got to my folks. Sorry guys. I have to watch it."

This kind of news is hard to fight. Your friends may grumble, or even get mean. Stand firm. They'll probably back off just enough for you to feel comfortable moving ahead.

Then get on with it as soon as you can. Your instincts are telling you this scene is not good for you. Listen to them. They come from the part of you that wants to keep you safe. They'll protect you, and give you strength, if you let them.

The great cheating dilemma

Chapter 3

There is no sense beating around the bush. The truth is that cheating is wrong. It's not the most awful of crimes, but it's dishonest and irresponsible, and in the end it does little good for anyone.

That said, let's take a look at the issues that complicate this basic truth. Why, since we all know cheating is wrong, do so many people do it in one form or another?

Part of the answer is that we only know what we allow ourselves to know. In other words, we can look at cheating in any number of ways. "I'm only helping a little," you might reason as you allow a good friend to take the answer to question number 5 off your paper. "I know the answer, I just forgot," you might assure yourself as you stealthily check and then slightly change one answer in accordance with your neighbor's. "This test is unfair. It serves Mrs. Simon right," you might declare silently as you slip a note from your pocket to check a list of World War II dates.

Still, whether or not people are willing to take responsibility for cheating, most know it's against the rules. Why, then, do those people go ahead and do it anyway?

The answer is simple. Because other issues seem more important at that moment. Other feelings, other people, other needs rule the situation. Cheating, while it is clearly wrong, simply doesn't seem wrong enough to stop us.

Is that so bad? you might ask. Can't there be exceptions? In some instances isn't cheating, well, necessary?

Perhaps the best answer to these questions is that there may not be a clear-cut answer. As you will see from the following situations, sometimes people simply have to make their own tough choices. They

have to decide what's right or wrong for them. They have to consider their values, listen to their hearts, consider their principles, and then reach a highly personal decision. In a way, cheating lends itself to this sort of deliberation. For one thing, cheating can sometimes feel downright useful. If you're copying, you might assume your grade will be higher. If someone is copying off of you, it might feel as if you're cementing a friendship. Also, since it's not a "crime" that can physically hurt someone, the choices often seem unclear. After all, you might think, who's getting hurt?

You might be surprised. The answer to that question is not so simple.

It's important to remember that to the outside world, to those not involved, the choices are not gray. They are black and white. Cheating is wrong; not cheating is right. If you cheat, then you must be willing to live with the consequences...which may be many.

Perhaps the most important thing to remember about cheating, beyond the right or wrong of it, is that cheating is a free ride for no one. It solves only the most momentary of problems. And it most often leaves everyone, at that moment, or sometime later, feeling used, confused, or downright unhappy.

So next time the temptation to cheat moves into the picture, think about it carefully. Consider everything. It's a far more complicated issue than you might think.

Friend asks to copy off your test

Q A good friend walks up to you the morning of a test and says, "I had a terrible fight with a friend last night and I couldn't study. Can I copy off your paper?" You've worked really hard, and you honestly would rather she didn't.

A Here is a perfect example of how knowing cheating is wrong doesn't necessarily add up to an easy answer.

There are a number of issues that may come into play as you make a decision. To begin with, is this an isolated instance? How often does your friend ask this of you? If this is a request she makes often, are you beginning to wonder if it's you she really likes or your grades? Do you think being a good friend would by definition require you to help her in this way, or do you think as a friend you might serve her better by refusing?

None of these are easy issues to face. But let's take a look at what your options might be in each situation.

If your friend rarely asks this of you, it will be especially hard to turn her down and you may not. If you decide to allow her access to your paper, however, you might clearly indicate that it doesn't make you happy. "I'm not going to stop you," you might say, "but it makes me nervous and a little upset. I know you're stuck," you might add in a sympathetic voice, "but I'm really uncomfortable about this." Answering her in this fashion will put the dilemma back on her shoulders, which is really where it belongs. In truth, why should you suffer all alone, in indecision, over *her* problem? You may feel that it would be selfish of you to refuse her,

but keep in mind that it's selfish of her to ask. Not every problem a friend shares with you needs to become your problem too.

If you decide you have to say no, you will want to explain why as sincerely as you can. "I'm really afraid we'll get caught, and besides, I studied really hard for this test. Please don't ask me to do this." Then you will want to offer her an alternative. In doing so you will be expressing your very real concern for her problem. Since it's rare that she needs to copy, it's likely that the teacher sees her as a reliable and responsible student as well. Why not suggest that she tell the teacher she's had a terribly upsetting night, and ask if it would be possible for her to take the test, or one just like it, the next day. Say that you will accompany her and support her story. Some teachers will go for this, some will not, but it's certainly worth a try. If this doesn't work, you might give her your notes that you studied last night and suggest she skip the class before the test to study them. (Make sure she speaks to someone in authority about this, such as a school counselor.) The point is to show that you do want to help her in some way and to give her the kind of help you can live with.

However, if this request to copy is chronic and annoying, it should be easier for you to say no. Still, do it with a clear explanation. It's not that you don't want to be friendly, it's that you think the situation is getting out of hand. "Not anymore. I'll help you study next time. Just ask. But I've worked hard and it bothers me to just give things away. It's not fair of you to always ask, either."

HELP!

My friend didn't do her math homework and wants to copy mine. It's the second time this week. It's starting to bother me.

Sure it's bothering you—you're doing all the work! Still, keep in mind your friend isn't gaining anything. In fact, she's losing. She isn't learning a thing, and when test time comes she's going to be in deep trouble. You should stop the pattern she's falling into, both for your sake and hers. Try telling her she can copy this assignment, provided the two of you go over it later so that when she attempts the next one on her own she'll be able to do it. This will honor her request, make it clear you want to help, and let her know she can't copy any more. You might also remind her that your teacher could pop a quiz. Chances are she'll start studying.

Of course, if your friend continually cheats off of you with your permission even though you don't like it, then the person with whom you really need to talk is yourself. Are you afraid of losing this person as a friend? Are you worried that grades are the only thing you have going for you? If so, it's critical that you realize no amount of shared papers or free answers will make a person like you. It will only make a person use you. You won't be buying affection. That's impossible. All you'll be getting is a "friend" who is cheating you out of the real thing.

Finally, are you afraid that to say no would indeed make you a terrible friend? After all, aren't friends supposed to be generous with each other? Yes, they are. But that doesn't mean that your friend's definition of generous must be yours. Your friend may think a good friend would let her copy. On the other hand, *you* might believe that a good friend wouldn't ask.

The trick is to believe in your own position. And you have to also realize that caring for a friend does not necessarily mean you have to do as she says or compromise your own stand. You *could* get caught cheating. Teachers, as you will see later in this chapter, are fairly adept at detecting suspicious test papers.

Good friends want to be there for each other. But it shouldn't mean they have a right to ask unfair things of each other, or to expect that when one of them thinks something is okay, the other should think so, too. Everyone is different. People view the same situation in myriad ways according to their own needs.

So the next time a friend says to you, "Can I cheat off your paper? I'm desperate!" stay calm. Be sympathetic. But remember you have a right to decide what will work for you. If she's a friend she'll live with your decision.

After all, cheating, no matter what side you're on, is no answer.

Caught cheating

Q You're unprepared for an algebra test, and so you copy a few answers off your friend's paper. She doesn't seem to mind. The next day your teacher asks the two of you to stay behind. Once the three of you are alone she says, "I finished grading the tests, and I have reason to believe there's been some cheating. Do you have anything to say?"

A The answer to that question should be "yes." Cheating, as you have just found out, is not simply dishonest, it's also a lit-tle dangerous. It can cast you in a negative light. It can hurt a basically innocent friend. And it can leave you feeling rather dirty.

The best way to survive getting caught is to admit your mistake. It will immediately make you look a little less dishonest. It will certainly clarify your friend's position. And you will definitely feel a lot cleaner if you speak the truth.

If you deny it in spite of what your teacher considers to be proof, she will have trouble ever trusting you again. And you will have created a situation in which you can't ask for academic help, because after all, you seemingly understand everything.

In the end, then, you lose anyway.

So be frank and brief. Don't hem and haw about your reasons. Don't look for sympathy, either. This may surprise you, but teachers actually feel a little hurt themselves when they catch students cheating. Some take it as a sign of disrespect toward them. Others worry about why you didn't learn the material to begin with, wondering if perhaps they didn't teach it well enough. So don't expect tenderness. Be matter-of-fact, truthful, and apologetic, even if you think your reasons for cheating sound pathetic.

♦ "I was scared all my answers were going to be wrong."
♦ "I didn't study carefully this time. I got caught up with other things."
♦ "I did study. I don't know, I just seemed to forget everything I knew. I got nervous with this test."
♦ "I never understood the material that well. I should have told you earlier. I'm sorry."

These answers may sound lame to you, but if they're the truth your teacher will keep them in mind as she considers what to do next. They will show your respect for her, and for yourself, too. They will let her know that you would not try to fool her a second time, and that you feel better being honest.

And then take the consequences without an argument. Your teacher may lower your grades considerably or make both of you take another test, or give both of you F's. In any event, you will likely want to firmly point out that your friend did not copy off of you, that this was *your* problem. Your teacher may or may not listen to this, however. In her view, you both were involved in the act of cheating, and since there's no way to determine who copied what, you should both be punished. If this happens you'll have learned a very serious lesson about cheating: It isn't a lone act. People get hurt.

One good thing about this situation is that you will likely not cheat again. Sometimes knowing right from wrong is not enough to stop people from making mistakes. But fear of getting caught is! The fear acts a bit like an internal policeman. It warns you against trying something dan-

HELP!

I didn't leave myself enough time to write a paper, and my friend, who's a year ahead, offered me the one she wrote last year.

What a temptation! The thing is, what if your teacher recognizes it? What if he senses it isn't yours because it doesn't sound like you? But worst of all, what if you get away with it? You'll have learned nothing, you'll get a grade you don't deserve, and while all your friends are feeling good or bad about how they did, you'll get to feel a little guilty and most likely a little dirty. Sure, the alternative is to rush through the paper and end up with a disappointing grade. But at least you'll deserve it. You won't feel good, but lying isn't going to feel better.

gerous. That internal police-man is a very helpful fellow when we are on the brink of taking chances we really shouldn't take. And cheating is a very big chance.

Teachers don't need to ac-tually catch you in the act to know cheating has taken place. They can see patterns of an-swers and compare them to seating charts. It isn't hard at all. They do it all the time, and not because they enjoy it. The teacher has a job to do. She has to teach and she has to stay aware of who is learning and who isn't. If she suspects

cheating, she has to face it head-on.

And if you're caught, so do you.

Then, once you've ac-cepted the punishment, you have to make some serious plans for catching up. If you admit to what you've done, your teacher will likely be very positive in her approach to helping you. She may at first check subsequent tests for signs of cheating, but in short order she will probably stop doing so. She will assume you've learned your lesson.

If you're caught cheating, just admit it. People make mis-takes. Cheating is an under-standable temptation. Teachers know this. They just don't like it and expect better from you.

Which, when you think about it, is a rather nice com-pliment.

Wrongfully accused

Q You are near the end of a hard history test and are feeling a bit anxious. You wonder how other people are doing. You pick up your head and start looking slowly around the room. Your eyes come to rest on your neighbor, who is furiously writing away. Suddenly you hear your teacher say to you, "Hand in your paper this minute!" Bewildered, you look up, only to realize she thinks you were cheating.

A Whatever you do, don't begin arguing with her from your seat. She won't want to hear it. She'll be too conscious of the other students in the class and will most likely shut you up immediately.

Instead, walk to the front of the class with your paper and try to softly explain that you were near the end of the test and simply looking around the room to see if your classmates were finishing up, too. (Everyone knows it's unsettling to finish a test only to discover everyone else is in the middle!) Tell her that if she'd just compare your answers with those of the kids sitting near you, she'd see you hadn't been copying. Your teacher may agree to this. If you have a reputation as an honest student, she will probably allow you to finish.

However, she may not. Perhaps there's been quite a bit of cheating in the class and she's tired of it. Perhaps you've been caught cheating before, or you simply haven't "clicked" with her very well this year; you haven't found her to be inspiring, and she has occasionally commented that you don't seem to be paying attention. She may insist that even if your answers are not identical, it seemed clear to her that you were staring at other people's work. And that, she might feel, is cheating, too.

Now, unfortunately, you have yourself a very difficult situation. Still, there are things you can do. First, you can suggest that she give you a kind of quiz, right then and there, or at the end of the day, so you can prove you know the mate-

rial. If this doesn't work, and she seems unwilling to give you a chance, ask to be excused from the classroom and go immediately to a school counselor. Describe what happened, including the offers you made to prove yourself. The counselor will almost certainly believe you (few students would have the nerve to go this far in defending themselves if they had been copying answers) and will probably contact your teacher.

The problem may resolve itself quickly. Your teacher might have been having a bad day, and she might have taken it out on you. When she's approached by the counselor, she may back down and give you the benefit of the doubt.

On the other hand, your teacher may point out that you shouldn't have been looking around. The counselor will have to agree with that. They may decide to test you again, or inform you that as a result of your actions, they will subtract the points missed due to questions that were not answered. Or your teacher might simply warn that she will be watching you carefully during future tests, and allow you to finish this last one.

As a result, you may elect to bring your parents into the picture. And probably, if they apply enough pressure, you will end up with the grade you'd have gotten if none of this had happened.

But before you call them in, keep this in mind. Unless this test is a midterm or a final, the truth is, it may not be worth the further discomfort that might arise between you

HELP!

I know that the person sitting next to me during a test copied the entire thing!

This can be absolutely enraging! Still, it happens. If this is a person with whom you have some sort of relationship, you might walk over and say, "Look, if you need help, ask me before the test. Please don't copy. It upsets me." There's certainly no point reporting it to the teacher. Doing so would only cast a bad light on you. The exception is if the teacher calls the two of you in because he sees similar mistakes on your papers. Then, of course, you must speak the truth.

If you don't know this person well, you can opt to tell him what you've heard and ask him not to do it again, or you can simply cover your test paper a little more carefully next time.

and your teacher. Anyway, face it—proper test behavior says keep your eyes on your paper, the clock, or the teacher, and that's all. Anything else can look very suspicious. If you have offered to take another test and gone to a school counselor, you will have made your position clear.

Finally, consider this. You have every right to defend yourself. But many times when a person is accused of doing something he didn't do, it's because of something he *did* do that was misunderstood. It's important to take stock of not just what we intend by our behavior, but also how it might be perceived. Taking responsibility for both things can keep you out of lots of trouble!

Plagiarized unknowingly

Q You've just gotten back a history paper you wrote on the causes of the Civil War. At least, you *thought* you wrote it. Scrawled across the top of the page, in bright red letters, are the words "See me. Do you know what the word 'plagiarize' means?" Your eyes travel down the first page and then the second. You stop there. An entire paragraph is circled in red.

To plagiarize means that you represent someone else's words as your own. It's that simple. It doesn't matter if you did it purposefully or innocently. If the words appear under your name and you fail to put it in quotes and note the source in some manner, then you are plagiarizing.

When you are called upon to write a research paper, the teacher expects that you will look up all the information you need in the proper sources (for instance, in magazines, newspapers, or encyclopedias) and then, in your own words, commit what you've learned to paper. This is not an easy matter. It can be very tempting to simply lift entire passages from a book and fit them into your own writing. It is so common, in fact, that students often do so not realizing what they've done. After all, when the essay is completed, it all sounds so good together!

Students fall into this trap partly because they haven't been trained properly. Perhaps in earlier grades, when teachers were paying more attention to things like spelling and punctuation than they were to the research, copied sentences were ignored or unnoticed. Now, these students suddenly find themselves in a position where more is expected. But old habits die hard. Also, perhaps some students mistakenly believe that if most of the paper is original, a copied paragraph here or there is fine. But that simply isn't so.

The best way to avoid plagiarizing is to refrain from writing a paper with the specific reference open before you. Write down the important pieces of information you need from a reference source into a notebook. Don't copy every word of every sentence. Rather, create a kind of shorthand. For example, the sentence "The day after the surrender of Fort Sumter, President Lincoln made a formal declaration of war and called for 75,000 volunteers" might be written into your notebook as "President L. declared war, day after surrender of Fort Sumter. Wanted 75,000 volunteers." Then put your references aside and study your notes. Organize the ideas. Finally, write the paper using your notes.

Naturally, if there is a particular passage that contains someone's idea or feeling, and it proves the point of your paper in a particularly powerful way, go ahead and use it. Just make sure you attribute it to that person either within the text of your paper or in a footnote.

What it gets down to is this: If you're going to write a paper, it has to be *your* paper—not someone else's. The teacher wants to know what you think, and he wants you to learn how to express yourself. He also wants you not to cheat.

Yes, plagiarism is cheating. It can take a slightly less deliberate form than copying an-

swers from someone else's test, but it has an equally dishonest result. Your name is attached to work that is not your own.

If you are found to have plagiarized something and you truly had not intended to, or you realized you were taking a paragraph but didn't think it mattered, just say so. Teachers recognize that this issue can sometimes be a confusing one. You will likely have to write that paper over again or create an entirely new one. Or you may have to accept a poor grade for the original paper. But do admit what must have happened.

Finally, understand that reading information and learning how to put it in your own words is an important skill. If it took a bad experience to illustrate the correct way to write a paper, you can live with that. Chances are you won't do it again.

"Changing" your report card

Q You've just gotten your report card and your grades are quite a bit worse than you expected. You know your parents will be very angry. They are bound to punish you, and so it seems you have only two choices. One, take a pen and change your grades, or two, take a pen and forge one of your parents' signatures.

A Actually, you have only one choice, and it's neither of the above. You must show your parents the report card. The most obvious reason for this is the honesty factor. But honesty may not be enough to keep you from doing *anything* you can to avoid your parent's disapproval.

So consider this.

You must show your parents the report card because the odds are overwhelming that you will get caught if you don't. You may think this isn't so, because friends have "confessed" they've successfully changed grades or forged signatures. Or you might have heard third or fourth hand that kids do it all the time and don't get caught.

But none of this, for the most part, is true.

First of all, your friends may not be telling you the truth. They may have intended to change a grade or forge a signature, but at the last moment changed their minds. They might tell you they've done so either to look "big" or to avoid having to admit to a punishment they'd rather find an excuse to explain away. ("My cousin is in from California so I have to go directly home after school for a week" sounds better than "My parents are making me come home after school to do my homework immediately!")

Second, when the lie is discovered, it's usually considered a very big deal at school. So big, that it's dealt with in a hush-hush serious way between teachers, the principal, and your parents. Your poor grades will pale next to the magnitude of the lie, and suddenly you will be looked at not simply as a student who has let his grades slip but as a student who is a liar and therefore cannot be trusted.

You don't want that. Suddenly everything you hand in will be suspect. Teachers will be wondering, is it your work? Did you copy it from someone?

You might wonder how your parents will find out. The answer is, any number of ways. One, your teacher may suspect the signature is not authentic. Two, your teacher may have expected a call from your parents after they see your grades, and when one is not forthcoming, may in fact call your parents himself. Three, your parents may wonder where the report card is.

Four, a final report card might reflect the poor grades, and even though the second part of the year saw some improvement, your parents may want to know what happened. (If you changed a grade before showing the card to your parents, your teacher will notice the changed grade either right away or later on if she uses the same card to write in your final marks.) Five, during a parent/teacher conference, the truth is bound to emerge.

Changing grades and forging signatures reflect the same lack of attention paid to future consequences as failing to do homework or study for tests. Both serve only the most immediate of purposes. Messing with your report card keeps your parents at bay only for a little while. And not studying for tests merely affords you a little more time with your friends. But down the line, your par-

ents will find out the truth, and your test results will be poor.

School is a place you attend in order to ensure a productive future. To do this you have to start small. You have to think ahead in all sorts of ways. You have to develop the self-discipline to study for tests, because your grades will come back to haunt you if you don't. And you have to face up to your mistakes, because to lie about them will afford you only temporary relief.

Everyone wants to find a way out of a tough spot as quickly as possible. It's natural to reach for what seems to be the easiest answer. But look again. Consider what could happen down the pike. And most of all, realize that most times the road to getting out of a jam is usually not an easy one. But, unlike a quick fix, it works in the long term, too.

Chapter 4

Grade grief

Grades are an issue for all students. No one, not even a straight-A student, is immune from worrying about them. Grades loom large every time you and your classmates sit down for a test, hand in a paper, take a quiz, or simply complete homework. The pressure can be constant.

Most kids, in fact, would rather see the entire grading system disappear and be replaced with a simple checkmark and a few supportive notes from the teacher!

But in truth, a grade is a good tool. It keeps students aware of how they're doing. It motivates them. It helps them judge where their strengths and weaknesses lie. It tells the teacher where a student needs more help. In short, grades are very informative.

Unfortunately, that's not the way you may view grades. Most students attach all sorts of hidden meanings to the score or letter at the top of the page. Some may think a poor grade means they're dumb. Others may feel good grades will win them friends, while poor grades will earn them rejection (or, even the other way around). And then there are those who see terrific grades as something to be embarrassed about, and poor grades as a kind of trophy (or vice versa).

In other words, depending on the individual student, grades are invested with a host of "magical" powers and messages.

And therein lies the big problem with grades. It's not what they really stand for that makes them difficult to swallow. What causes the real trouble are the things students believe they mean.

For example, if you get a poor grade on a math test, and can honestly determine you simply didn't study hard enough or that there was a basic concept you misunderstood, then you can fix it! You can study harder, get a little

extra help, and find yourself right back on track with higher grades. But if you believe a poor grade on a math test means you're dumb, then where is there to go? Well, how about into a dark room with a sign on the door reading, HOPELESS: I GIVE UP!

Add into the mix that grades are often a subjective matter, and things really get complicated. What one teacher considers an A paper might only rate a B from another teacher. So what does that mean? A person is only as smart as the particular classroom he or she happens to be sitting in? How ridiculous!

The goal of this chapter is to get you back to basics. Grades are not a crystal ball, reflecting back the "truth" about your intelligence or capabilities. Grades are a flawed but workable way for you and your teachers to assess how well you are learning at a particular time. Certainly one can draw the conclusion that if you do well you must be quite bright. But it does not follow that if you don't do well you aren't.

There are a host of reasons why students might run into troublesome grades (including having a poor teacher!), and there are many ways to cope with and improve the situation. The important thing is to view the grade for what it is—and not what it isn't.

It's a judgment call about your work.

Not about you.

Unfair grade

Q Last week you proudly handed in a book report you were sure deserved an A. It's just been returned to you, however, with a big red B– scrawled across the top. You are terribly upset, and absolutely sure you've been graded unfairly.

It's possible. The grade may be a harsh one. Another teacher might have judged the paper differently. But given the difference between what you expected and what you received, chances are there are some problems with your work. The most important concern right now is knowing what they are. To ignore the problem would only leave you open to yet another disappointing grade.

Try and live with your reaction for a day or two. Give the intense disappointment and anger you quite naturally feel a little time to cool down. Then go back and study the paper. Consider your teacher's comments (if there are any). Now that you have a little distance, her remarks may seem to have a point. Reread what you have done and see if you can better understand why you received a grade considerably lower than the one you had expected.

If you honestly continue to feel that you deserved a bet-ter grade, make an appointment with your teacher. Don't just drop in. She might be busy and thus be unable to hear you out fully. Tell her that you have something you need to discuss, and ask when a convenient time might be. Make sure you appear promptly at the appointed time and that you bring your paper with you.

Begin by making it clear that you are confused—not that she is wrong, or that you are angry. Ideally, your teacher will appreciate your concern over your paper, but she may not. The two of you may not have clicked this year, or she may be a person who doesn't like to be challenged. So proceed carefully and remember that your teacher is just a person, too. No one likes to be attacked or accused of wrongdoing. "Mrs. Ryan, I am concerned about my book report. I enjoyed the book so much, and I really felt I had some important things to say about it. I thought I did that really well. But I can see from your grade that you didn't think so."

Next, listen very carefully. Your teacher will likely go through the work with you pointing out the weaknesses. Try and hear her with as objective an ear as you can. Don't let your emotions get in the way. If you feel uncertain about any points she is making, go over them again with her. If at the conclusion of this part of the discussion you still feel that you deserved better than the mark you received, ask her to explain in detail the criteria she uses when arriving at a specific mark. For a book report she may be looking at spelling, organization, clarity of thought, and factual content. Be sure and pay attention. She is telling you more than just what she focuses on when reviewing a paper—she is also telling you what to focus on when you are writing one!

Chances are, at the conclusion of this meeting you will have a pretty fair idea of why you received a particular grade. Then again, there's always the possibility (though not the most likely one!) that your discussion will conclude with your teacher improving your grade. She may listen to what you have to say, reread a section here or there, and conclude she may have been too tough on you.

That would be nice.

But it's not the most important thing. The truth is, the book report is only one paper. You'll have plenty more to hand in and they will probably reflect an improvement. You now understand what your teacher is looking for, and you can apply that knowledge to any future assignment. The next time you hand in a paper thinking it's worth an A, there's a better chance she'll agree.

The slow class

Q You've gotten another poor grade on a math test and your teacher suggests it's time for you to try a class that moves a little less quickly. You're terribly embarrassed and feel hopelessly dumb.

A First of all, try to remember that you, like everyone else, have your strengths and weaknesses. No one can do everything well. Certainly, being forced to confront an apparent weakness can make you feel badly. But that weakness is just a small part of a much more important and very capable whole you.

Second, try and understand why teachers might decide you would do better in a class that moves more slowly. It's not that he thinks you're dumb, or will never do well in a subject, or couldn't under any circumstances keep up with a faster class.

Most often a teacher suggests that you take a class that moves at a more regulated pace so that you can feel more comfortable and confident. It is common knowledge that a person who feels pressured and tense will not learn as easily or as well as someone who is relaxed and self-assured. The problem with dragging grades for most students is that they are hard to change.

This is partly because as each unsatisfactory grade appears, it eats away little by little at a student's confidence. Pretty soon, he or she can start to believe, "I just can't do it." That in turn sometimes brings students to the point where they just stop trying.

By changing your class the teacher hopes a number of things will happen. One, if the subject hits your weak spot, the new class will make it possible for you to comfortably keep up and learn in a relaxed fashion. Two, if it's simply a matter of you having gotten stuck in an unfortunate pattern, the teacher is hoping the new class will give you an opportunity to go back and learn something you missed, or relearn something you misunderstood. Then, if everyone agrees, you might be returned to the more quickly paced class ... though you may decide you'd rather not go!

But more than anything, your teacher is anxious for you to get the most out of class. Yes, it can feel bad if someone says to you, "Look. I think you're having trouble keeping up." But consider this. Doesn't it feel worse constantly receiving low grades when it seems you're working as hard as you can? And won't you feel better attending a class in which you understand what's going on than one in which you are completely lost?

Which brings up a final point. Many kids label one class the "smart" class, and another the "dumb" one. This is cruel and inaccurate. There are plenty of students with plenty of brains who simply have trouble with math or English or French or biology or you-name-it! They may do well in some classes and rather poorly in others. It has to do with the things that interest them and the kind of thinking they do best. Some people are very creative thinkers. They might write beautifully. Others are logical thinkers. They might be strong math students. Still others are talented analytical thinkers. They might do particularly well in economics.

But a good English student who isn't that comfortable with math is not dumb. He simply writes better than he computes. To put it another way, he's human.

In an advanced class

Q You've just been placed in an advanced English class, and suddenly you're surrounded by some of the smartest kids in your grade. You've always been a good writer, but the idea of sitting side by side with these brains is terrifying. Also a little annoying. You've been receiving A's in the regular English class, and now you fear your grade average will go downhill.

A Congratulations! Your teacher has elected to place you in an advanced class because he or she feels you can handle more difficult work. Whether or not you stay in the class, whether or not you maintain your A average, and whether or not you can cope with the anxiety this challenge brings, you should commend yourself. Someone out there in a posi-

tion to know thinks you do strong work.

Now, what about that anxiety? What exactly is it telling you? On the surface maybe a sign that you're thinking, "Uh-oh! I'm not as smart as these guys. What am I doing here?" or "I don't think I can do this work!" But that's just the surface. That's just putting words to a feeling so that you can understand the feeling better. But the truth is, anxiety doesn't have to mean that. It doesn't have to mean you're in the wrong place. Anxiety can be a very natural and even a very helpful response to a challenge. It can be the driving force behind you working harder and better and meeting the many challenges put before you.

In short, anxiety can actually spur you on to do very good work. It operates like a motor, propelling you forward.

Of course, it can also have the opposite effect.

Sometimes students experience so much anxiety over their work that their performance suffers. The anxiety gets in the way of their ability to absorb information, or to think clearly, or to work carefully, and as a result they appear unable to keep up— which is, of course, exactly what they feared. It's a very unfortunate vicious cycle, because the trouble is not born of inability; it's born of the destructive side of anxiety.

If you believe your anxiety is getting in your way, try and talk it through with either your teacher or a school counselor or psychologist. You might be having an acute case of "performance anxiety," and if you deal with it directly, it may begin to pass. If it doesn't, you can always ask to be returned to your original class. But save that as a last resort. There will be many times in your life when you will be called upon to rise to a challenge. You can't go through life refusing to give tough things a shot for fear of failing. For one thing, you'll be cheating yourself out of a lot of possible glory! At some point you're going to have to say to yourself, "I'm afraid, but I'm going to do my best and that will have to be enough." And you're going to have to do this because you will only know true self-satisfaction if you strive to move forward. If you continue to be dogged by this tendency to run, you might need to seek some help or support from a parent, teacher, or counselor.

Which brings us to the issue of breaking your A record. Here's a piece of information you should keep in mind. An A record in a regular

H E L P !

I've just been moved into an advanced math class in the middle of the term, and my first homework assignment is way too hard!

Not surprising. Probably the class is ahead of you. That doesn't mean you don't belong, it just means you have some catching up to do. Speak to your teacher, see if you can get into a study group with some of the other students, and don't expect too much of yourself. You're in this class because your teacher feels you have a strong ability in math and can handle the challenge—not because he assumes you know everything that has already been covered. No one said you were Einstein, did they?

class is less impressive than a B record in an advanced class. That's a fact. Sure, it sounds good to tell someone you have an A average in one subject or another. But if someone is reviewing your school record to see if you are an appropriate candidate for a special summer program or even a particular college, he or she will note with great interest and respect that you were enrolled in an advanced class and that you received solid grades for your efforts.

The bottom line? Don't be afraid to challenge yourself. Obviously you've shown a special ability or you would not have been selected for the class. But don't give it a try because you feel you have to live up to what others expect. That's how the anxiety can get overwhelming. Rather, do it for yourself. See how well you can do. And expect to have a tough time.

That's what good challenges are all about.

Difficult test

Q You've just finished taking a test you thought was way too difficult. You are sure you understood the material quite well. You're terribly upset and are thinking about approaching the teacher when the period is over to complain about the questions.

A Don't do it!
This is a very common experience with many possible explanations. Before you complain you need to sort out what might have happened and then wait out the results.

First of all, and most obvi- ously, you might not have understood the material as well as you thought. Sometimes one or two basic confusions can lead to all sorts of trouble on a test. (This is particularly true with math.) Perhaps you didn't study quite hard enough or you did study but you concentrated on the wrong things. Before you can complain that a test is too hard, you need to honestly assess if you were as prepared as you thought.

Another possibility is that the test *was* very hard. And that in fact *everyone* thought so. In that case, everyone's grade will reflect the level of difficulty. The teacher will likely then score the test "on a curve," which means that while a 95 might have meant an A if the test was simple, an 85 might now rate an A. Before you complain, ask around. See what your friends thought. Then wait for the grades to come out. You might be pleasantly surprised.

Finally, consider this. Difficult tests are part of the school experience. Sure, they can be outrageously tough, but they're a fact

of school life. Some teachers are tougher on grades than others. Some papers are harder to write than others. And some tests are more difficult than others. Of course, a lot of how difficult things seem depends on your particular strengths and weaknesses. You may have a personality clash with a teacher and so she seems tough. You may be better at computation than at writing papers. And multiple-choice tests might be a much better bet for you than short-answer tests.

As for what to do if you alone had a problem? Talk to your teacher and do whatever you can to catch up. You're not the first student to stumble on a test. Accept the experience for what it is—a test meant to indicate how well you understand the material, not how smart you are.

Essay writing

Q There's a big history exam coming up and you are not a very good writer. You'll do fine on the true/false questions and fill-in-the-date section. But when it comes to essays, you just seem to fall apart. It almost feels like there's no point in trying.

A Good writing skills are critical. There's no way around that. And anyone can have them. Not everyone can have "a way with words." Not everyone can be an author. But everyone can and must learn good, basic writing skills. Today it's essays and papers. Later on it will be college admission forms, then job applications and résumés, and then, further down the pike, business reports and correspondence. No matter what you do in life now, or later, it's critical that you learn to express yourself on paper.

So, of course, you have to keep trying. But you have to do so with a plan.

You have to give the skill of writing the respect and attention it deserves. You have to think through the task at hand, understanding fully that you must be able to put forth your ideas in a clear, well-developed manner so that someone reading your paper will know precisely what you think, and why.

You can do that. It simply takes time and discipline. What you need to do is schedule a special meeting with your history or English teacher in order to get specific help. You might even, if it's financially possible, ask your parents to get you a tutor who can help you strengthen your writing skills. Also, there are probably several books in your school library that would serve as strong guides.

Essay writing is not the big mystery it can seem to be. Assuming you can spell decently and you know how to construct a sentence, your primary job is to train your brain to think in a logical way. It goes something like this.

An essay usually has a point. What's yours? Whatever it is, that's your lead sentence. Now, since you want people to believe you, you have to explain why you think

HELP!

I can't remember details on tests! Dates, names, and vocabulary words just fly out of my head!

Lots of people have trouble with this. What you need is a bag of tricks! You need some "personal prompters" to help you remember all the facts. For instance, the French word for library is *la bibliothèque*. Can't remember that? Imagine yourself in the library eating a lobster. You'll need a bib. It's a ridiculous thought, but it's less likely to leave your mind than the actual word. When you take the test, you'll remember that image, and once you have the word *bib* in your head, the word *bibliothèque* will follow.

your point is true. On a separate piece of paper, list all the reasons you think you are correct. Then organize those reasons in whatever way proves your point best. You might need to order your reasons, for example, in accordance with when each thing occurred. Next, take this information and put it into paragraph form. Then, finally, sum up. Pull out your most important points, and rephrase your very first sentence with a little more detail.

If your lead sentence is, "I believe that all porcupines would dance better if they lived in Texas," and you go on to explain why, then your concluding sentence might be, "Purple rainbows, affectionate snakes, and ten gallon hats make Texas the perfect state for dancing porcupines." (Clearly this is a joke, but you get the point.)

You may never be a world-famous author. You may never be the best writer in your class. You might be at your most expressive in front of an easel, or simply in conversation. But just because you may not be able to turn a phrase in a poetic way, or you find that it's a struggle to formulate your thoughts on a piece of paper, that doesn't mean good writing skills are beyond your ability.

Fire fighters need to write reports.

Computer programmers need to write instructions.

Builders need to write proposals.

And just about everyone finds himself, at one time or another, having to write a letter of complaint, a note to a teacher, a request for information, an addendum to a contract, a will, a note of apology, a message of thanks, a petition, a love letter, and all sorts of other written material.

So will you. School is your opportunity to work hard on your writing skills. Take advantage of it now, so that later, when it's time to write what you mean, you don't first have to learn how to write.

Nervous test-taker

Q You panic on tests. The night before, you usually feel a little sick, and by the time the test is before you, it seems as if you have forgotten everything you studied. You blank. Once you begin working, you relax a little, but because of your anxiety, you don't do as well as you should.

A The most important thing to keep in mind about a test is what it *doesn't* measure. It doesn't measure your intelligence. It doesn't measure your potential. And it doesn't measure your future performance.

A test only measures to what degree you can *prove*

you have mastered the material covered by the test. You may know much more than comes across. You may simply be a poor tester.

If you are, you're not alone.

Test taking is not an easy task. Even if you accept that a poor grade doesn't make you stupid, it doesn't feel good to be tested. To have to prove yourself. To have to display your strengths, on command, knowing you are being judged.

Lots of people experience anxiety when they have to perform. As a result, they often don't perform as well as they might have had the pressure not been on.

But the truth is, throughout your life you will find yourself "onstage." There will be moments when you have to display what you know—and, yes, what you don't know. Some people love the challenge. Others don't. But since we all have to do it, you are going to have to find a way to control your anxiety so that at

the very least it doesn't interfere with the job at hand.

Here are some suggestions for cooling yourself out before the big test:

◆ Don't drive yourself crazy the night before! Start studying a few nights before the test so that everything isn't left to the last minute. Cramming doesn't stick anyway. You'll be far more likely to remember information if you give yourself time for it to sink in.

◆ Consider what will happen if you don't do well. This is a very interesting thing to do, because most often people discover that the consequences of doing poorly actually don't match their degree of anxiety. Certainly it would be unpleasant to score poorly, but a clear look at the consequences will help you avoid working yourself up into an unnecessary near-crisis state.

- A poor grade might mean you need to go back and relearn some material. That's not so bad.
- A poor grade might mean

your overall grade for the year could be dragged down. That's not so bad, either, given that your teacher may decide to balance things differently if you begin to improve.

- A poor grade may mean you have to work extra hard the rest of the year. That's not the worst thing!
- And finally, a poor grade might mean you'll catch

My friend and I studied everything together for the history test. But she got a B and I got a C+. What happened?

She did better. Maybe she recalled more facts on her essay than you did on yours. Maybe you got careless with a date or two. Maybe she enjoys tests and you don't.

Maybe, maybe, maybe. It doesn't matter. It's a waste of time wondering why you and your friends can't stay neck and neck in the "great grade race." You shouldn't be competing with each other. What's most important is that you keep trying to better your performance. If you got a C+ and feel you could have or should have done better, then find out what you did wrong. Work on the problem. Try to do better next time, and stop worrying about how your friends do. They don't look like you, talk like you, laugh like you, think like you, or enjoy every last thing that you enjoy. So why, really, should you ever score exactly the same?

some flak from your parents. That, too, ought to be manageable, especially if your grades improve.

When you look at it this way, a poor grade on a test is an extremely surmountable problem. Here's how:

◆ Do what is known as a "visualization" exercise. Sit in a quiet room and close your eyes. Imagine taking your seat in the class and being handed the test. Look down at that test. See it for what it is—simply a piece of paper upon which you'll write down your answers. Now, imagine a specific question to which you know the answer. In your mind's eye, pick up your pencil and begin writing. Or if you'd rather, just imagine the page quickly filling with your handwriting as you confidently write down what you know.

The point of this kind of exercise is to give yourself a chance to play the same scene differently. It doesn't have to

be a nightmare. It can be an opportunity to shine. Paint yourself into the picture positively and keep doing it over and over. Rehearse success. Don't just entertain vague fears.

◆ Right before the test, try and find a quiet spot to do some deep-breathing. (Look for an empty classroom, or perhaps try the cafeteria if it's off-hours.) Anxiety can make your whole body go into high gear. Your heart may be pumping too hard. Your breathing may be too short, and you might even break into a sweat. It can be very uncomfortable and can actually interfere with your thought processes. You ought to get some oxygen into your system. It will relax your muscles and clear your mind.

◆ If your friends tend to get anxious as well, or if they have

Help! My teacher hates me

a habit of testing each other at the last minute, avoid them. That kind of frenzied activity will only make you more nervous. Your mind is likely to blank when they ask you a question, and if that happens you may panic. Their companionship isn't worth the stress!

◆ If your anxiety level still feels high as you are doing the test, take a few deep breaths. If you can't remember the answer to a question, just move on. Don't beat yourself up or make more of it than it's worth. Thoughts such as "Oh, no! What am I going to do?" or "What if I can't answer everything else, too?" are simply destructive and silly. Answer the questions you are sure of so that your confidence can build.

Then go back and slowly work your way through the difficult questions.

Tests are not a reflection of your worth. But they can reflect your nerves.

Don't let this happen to you. If you're going to get a poor grade, do so because you just didn't know the answer, and not because you were too nervous to think it through.

Note: There are professionals trained in techniques to help you reduce anxiety. I've sketched out a few of their methods here. If you try these and still don't feel an improvement, speak to your parents. Your school psychologist could refer you to someone to help you learn these skills.

Handling great grades

Q Your grades have been terrific. So good, in fact, that you are embarrassed in front of your friends. You're afraid they will either tease you unmercifully or actually not want to hang around you anymore because somehow they'll see you as different.

A Your good grades should not be a problem for anyone, least of all you.

Still, some kids are threatened by those who do very well in school. They may feel envy, desperately wishing they could do as well. They may feel fear, worrying they are simply not as smart. They may feel resentment, wondering how it is you don't mind being "uncool" with your smart-kid profile. And most of all, they may feel defensive, obsessed with the notion that you think you're too good for them.

But not all kids feel this way. Some of it has to do with who they are, and some of it with how you handle your success. Revealing in a relaxed, non-self-congratulatory way that you're doing well will likely not bother many kids.

But grandly brandishing a straight-A report card will likely earn you a few enemies.

There are ways to be honest about how you're doing that will not frighten or offend. But before you employ them, you have to get straight, inside yourself, about what's really going on for you.

It is very natural to want to fit in. Belonging to a group with whom you have a lot in common can feel terrific. But only if you're being honest with yourself and others.

Lying about who you are, or keeping an important part of yourself under wraps for fear of what your friends will think, will only end up making you unhappy.

This is not to say that you need to reveal everything about yourself in the name of honesty. Not at all. The issue is *why* you choose to keep certain information about yourself to yourself. Perhaps you view certain things as very private. That's your right. But if it's because you are afraid you will no longer be liked, then you have a problem.

Either you are underestimating your friends or they may not be the friends you think they are. In either case, you owe it to yourself to find out. You can only be who you are. There's no point wasting time hanging out with kids who would reject you if they knew "the truth."

So the next time you get an A and a friend asks you how you did, try saying, "I did well," with a smile. If he presses you for the details, tell him. Don't belabor it. He'll think you're obnoxious. Don't apologize for it. He'll think you're talking down to him. And don't dismiss it as an accident. He'll know you're a phony.

And if your friend tries to lay guilt on you for being a do-gooder, or teases you for being a "teacher's dream," bluntly inform him that you will not answer any more questions about your grades. He'll just have to guess. If he really likes you, he'll get the point.

Chapter **5**

Homework
hang-ups

Probably doing homework is not your favorite thing. This is certainly understandable.

Not only can it be very difficult and time-consuming, it can eat away at your social life and leave you feeling confused and frustrated. A teacher can heap it on as if he thinks his is the only class you're taking. Joint projects can ruin friendships and lone projects can seem overwhelming.

And that's only part of it. You have to understand the assignment, listen in class so that you have the skills to do the homework, allot enough time to get it done after school, do it neatly and to the best of your ability, remember to bring it in (if it's written), and then, do all of this on a daily basis.

Just thinking about it is exhausting.

Still, incredibly, homework does not exist just to annoy you!

Homework is an important way for you to move through your grade's curriculum. You can't cover everything in class. There just aren't enough school hours, and you couldn't sit that long if there were! Homework is an opportunity for the day's lesson to sink in, and also for you to learn material that you can study on your own. It's also a chance for you to learn to work well with others.

You don't need your teacher in front of you every moment to further your education.

Nor would you want her there!

Homework is, quite simply, another chance for you to learn. The thing is, though, it's not optional. So, given that homework is a given, and that it's really not a bad thing (or at least the point of it isn't!), how can you approach the assignments more positively?

The trick is surrender. Homework should not be an enemy with whom you have to regularly do battle. For one thing, you won't win that way! You'll resent it, you won't do as well as you could, you may lose it, forget it, and just plain muck it up. Homework is here to stay, and you'll do a lot better if you just make room for it in your life.

You may need to draw up a schedule for your after-school hours so that you leave enough time for a certain number of subjects each day. Also, to make sure homework will not simply gobble up your life, leave time on that schedule for "play time." Write the words in red if you'd like! When depression hits, it will pop out at you every time.

Take it easy on yourself. Sometimes things happen in life that make work difficult. Sad, exciting, or just plain unexpected things can occur, and suddenly homework assignments can't get done.

You're entitled to those times. But don't allow yourself to get lost in them. Remember, homework is part of your learning. It's not a punishment (despite the way it may sometimes feel). If you miss doing some homework, you've missed learning something. And since most assignments build on each other, you will likely need to find the time to squeeze it in later.

Your teacher won't always know if you've done your work. But *you* will.

That's the other thing about homework. It's a measure of your own desire to move forward. It's not necessarily the grade. Lots of homework isn't graded.

It's a question of what it is *you* want from school.

Help at home

Q Before handing in your progress report on a science experiment you are conducting at home, you asked your mother to read it over and make suggestions. She did, and you improved on your report. But now you don't feel so good. Your teacher handed it back, and after telling you it was excellent work, has asked if you got help from your parents. You feel very mixed-up and guilty . . . as if you did something wrong.

First of all, this is not a nice question, though certainly teachers have been known to ask it. The reason you really feel upset is that the question has an insulting silent message (even if your teacher doesn't mean it that way). That message is, "This is so good I can hardly believe you did it by yourself."

But of course you *did* do it by yourself. Asking for helpful suggestions to improve something is a completely acceptable part of doing a project on one's own. In fact, it's a very intelligent way to make sure that you have brought as much to the work as possible.

As for what to do when asked this question, there are two things you could do wrong in this situation. One, say you got help without explaining the nature of that assistance, and two, confuse in your own head the difference between asking for help and asking someone else to do your homework. The best answer is "My parents gave me ideas for improving this, but I did all the work myself."

It is perfectly all right to ask a parent, an older sibling or a good friend, or a tutor to help you with your homework. However, let's be clear about how we are defining the word *help*. Asking someone to look over your work and suggest ways to strengthen it is fine, as long as you do the strengthening. Handing someone your work and asking them to fix it is *not* fine. Asking someone to explain how you might approach a problem is fine. Handing someone the problem and asking them to "get you started" or "do the first part" is not. Asking someone to point out where you made some mistakes is fine. Handing someone your paper and asking them to correct your work is not.

It's really a question of who does the work. Your teachers, in fact, will be very pleased if they know there is someone at home who cares enough to review the work that they have begun with you.

In fact, the two reasons it's important to tell your teacher, "Yes, I got help, and this is how . . ." are one, it's the truth, and two, it's a way for her to judge your progress and be more aware of the areas in which you do need help.

Needing support to complete homework assignments is not a crime! So don't act like it is. You have nothing to hide. You knew enough to ask for advice and were lucky enough to have someone around who could advise you!

Undone homework

Q You had a terrible misunderstanding with a few friends the other night. You haven't been able to concentrate on anything since, including your homework assignments. Then in class, your teacher called on you to answer a question about last night's reading. Since you didn't do it, you didn't know what to say.

A A lot of how this situation works itself out will depend on the kind of student you were before all of the trouble started.

Obviously, if you were never particularly reliable the teacher will have trouble accepting or having sympathy for your story, even if it is true. This is not to say you don't deserve understanding during this difficult time. It just means it may be a little harder to come by.

Nevertheless, no matter what your history in the classroom, it's best to handle this situation in a straightforward, honest manner. You might be tempted to try and guess at an answer, but don't do it. It will only increase the amount of attention paid to you, and will make it seem as if you're try-ing to trick your teacher, which in a way you are.

Rather, simply say, "I'm sorry. I couldn't get to my work last night. I'll catch up tonight." Chances are, rather than waste any more time, the teacher will move on to an-other student, and she will move on for another reason as well.

She knows things happen. Any number of unex-pected things can occur in any given day that make it difficult

HELP!

I didn't do my homework yesterday because I just got too busy with other stuff. When the teacher asked me why I didn't know what to say.

Try, "I have no excuse. I'm sorry. I'll get it done and hand it in tomorrow." Your teacher won't be happy, and you won't feel proud, but it's the truth and it's not a tragedy. Everyone has days when they simply don't ac-complish what they should. Even teachers. Just don't make a habit of it. "I have no excuse," is acceptable once. Twice, you might squeak by. A third time, and those words will fall on deaf, very annoyed ears.

if not impossible for us to meet all of our responsibilities. It is, in principle, acceptable that you were unable to complete an assignment. After all, many teachers go home expecting to grade papers, only to have something come up that makes it impossible for them to do so.

Your teacher may let it go at this without requiring any further explanation from you. Or, depending on whether this has become a pattern with you or whether or not your mood has visibly changed over the past few weeks, she may take you aside after class and ask if something is bothering you.

HELP!

I've fallen behind in my reading assignments and now a test has just been announced. I'm in a panic!

Don't panic. It will get in your way. There is probably still time to correct the problem. You will likely have to trade in some fun time in order to catch up, but that's the way it goes. Make a plan. Divide the number of pages you have to study by the number of nights you have left to work. Study the allotted pages each night. If you try to cram too much into your head in one night, it won't stick. You may have to let some parts of another class assignment slip in order to squeeze in preparation for this test. If so, keep a chart of what's passed you by so that as soon as the test is over you can go back and catch up. In other words, expect that you will be feeling the effects of having let so much work go undone, even after the test.

In a short time you should have your homework

Whether or not your teacher asks if you're troubled by something, you might want to consider telling her on your own. In this case it's an argument with some friends. Another time you might find there are some upsetting problems at home. Whatever the problem, letting

it out should help, as she will more readily understand if your work is late or not quite up to par. Of course, you may not want to tell her very much at all and so her question might make you uncomfortable. You have a right to your privacy. Other than to acknowledge that you must keep your work up, you do not owe your teacher an in-depth personal explanation for your sagging grades. You need to find the words, however, to explain yourself. Here are some suggestions.

schedule back on track. And this time, maybe, you'll decide to stay on top of it!

Note: If you haven't been keeping up and your teacher suddenly announces, "Take out a piece of paper. We're having a quiz," then you are just out of luck. But only this time. Do the best you can, and then work some extra study hours into your schedule in order to catch up. Hopefully this quiz won't do anything to your final grade that a good score on the follow-up test can't fix.

♦ "There are some problems I'm having at home, but I can't talk about them now. I'll work hard to catch up."
♦ "I'm having some problems with friends, but if you don't mind I'd rather not discuss them. I'm sorry about the work. I'll try to do better, but I might need some help."
♦ "I've been very upset about some things that I feel funny talking about. I know I need to do better with my work."

Chances are, your teacher will accept your need for privacy but will also suggest that you talk to a school counselor or psychologist. You should give this serious consideration.

Even though it's understandable that you would not want to discuss your problems with just anyone, there's a risk involved when you sit on a pile of problems without getting any help with the difficult emotions they inspire. Your sadness, anger, or fear can begin to negatively affect all areas of your life. You might fight more with friends. You might get very angry over little things, or cry over almost nothing. And your schoolwork is bound to suffer.

The important thing is not the work, though. It's how you feel.

What matters is finding a way for you to cope during this difficult time so that your life stays on track. Once you get the emotional support you need and gain a better understanding of what is bothering you, everything else in your life will be easier to manage. (It's possible you are arguing with friends because something else you aren't aware of is distressing you.)

This doesn't mean that every time someone upsets you it's okay to sit back and forget your responsibilities. Not at all. Difficult things happen to everyone, and we can't just throw up our hands and say, "Well, that's it. I'm not doing a thing till I feel better." But sometimes, despite our best efforts, we just can't manage everything.

This happens to everyone.

Let your teacher know that it's happening to you.

And if for some reason she doesn't get it, or even if she does, think about speaking to a counselor at school. Some teachers simply lack the skills necessary to give students the help they need.

You have a right to the understanding, patience, and support of your school. You just have to ask for it.

Oral reports

Q You are petrified of public speaking. To-morrow is your turn to stand up and give an oral report, but the very thought of staring into your classmates' faces is making you break into a sweat. What if you can't speak? What if you forget everything? What if you make a fool of yourself?

A Keep two things in mind:

One, almost everyone feels the same way you do, even after they've had lots of practice!

Two, you are not expected to be able to give a speech with *savoir faire* (that is, grace and confidence). That's why you're studying public speaking.

The trouble with learning the skill of public speaking is that one has to learn it in public! Almost everything else you endeavor to learn can be done in relative privacy. If you don't quite get a step in algebra, the whole class will not be aware of your poor homework paper. If your book report is not up to par, only you and your teacher need know about it. But when it comes to public speaking, it feels as if all your classmates have their eyes on you and your performance.

And actually, they do.

But those eyes, which to you look *so* critical, are in fact no such thing. Rather, they probably reflect a great deal of sympathy, anxiety, and, yes, relief. It's you up there, not them, and thank goodness you look as nervous as they feel.

You may think your classmates are just waiting for you to slip, but they're probably just sitting there dreading their own turn. (If they do hope you slip it's because they figure they won't look so bad if they do the same.)

You might think making a mistake will make you look stupid, but it won't. Confused, perhaps. Nervous, most likely. Everyone knows that public speaking shakes the confidence of even very smart people.

You may be terribly embarrassed if you start to sweat, or if your voice shakes or if your hands tremble, but give yourself a break! Anyone noticing your anxiety will understand and feel comforted that you are reacting the same way they do.

And as for those classmates who may snicker when you stutter, or whisper when you shake, or smile when you forget a fact—don't be fooled! People who laugh at others' weak moments do so because they are afraid of their own. They're glad someone can feel as insecure as they do. They're relieved to see a person bend under pressure, much the same way they do. The smiling, whispering, and laughing come from their need to feel bigger and better when they really feel smaller and much less good.

In terms of how you can prepare for public speaking, the best thing to do is rehearse. Do it by yourself in front of a mirror, or in front of a friend, or even in front of more than one friend if you can. Also, try some visualization. As you rehearse, imagine yourself speaking in front of only a person or two. Then add a few more. And then some more. You will probably feel some anxiety as you do this, but it will give you an opportunity to get used to the feeling even as you continue to speak. This will help a lot when the real moment arrives.

It's important to put together clean, easy-to-scan notes. Whether you choose to use index cards or notepaper to prompt yourself, make sure the print is clear and the phrases far enough apart so that your eye can catch the words you need. A bad case of nerves will make it hard to both concentrate on what you're saying and focus on the words you've jotted down. So minimize the problem. Bring clean, clear notes with you to the front of the class. (You'll want to discuss with your teacher the form these notes

should take. One teacher might allow an entire speech to be written out. Another might prefer simple phrases. And still another might urge that you come prepared with only an outline.)

Above all else, however, do keep in mind that public speaking is a learned skill. You aren't born with the ability to get up in front of a group of people and express yourself.

But remembering that every person watching and listening is worrying about his or her performance should help you out a lot. In fact, some may be so worried about their own turn that they're probably not even listening to you at all!

Which, after all the work you put into the presentation, could actually be ever so slightly annoying . . . believe it or not.

Lazy project partner

Q You and a partner are supposed to be working on a class project together. You have three weeks within which to complete the assignment, and you're working very hard to do so. The trouble is, he isn't, and as a result you're working double-time and yet still falling behind. You're so angry you could explode.

A Who can blame you? You have a partner. He's supposed to carry his fair share of the load. He isn't, and it is creating a problem. You are doing most of the work, and yet in all likelihood your grade will suffer because the project is not as good as it might have been.

You must talk to your partner. But do so with a little social savvy.

No one likes to be attacked. No one likes to be threatened or accused. And no one likes to feel like a bad person. If they do, they will pour most of their energies into defending themselves instead of listening to you. Then, of course, nothing gets solved and everyone leaves the conversation feeling miserable.

Besides, there's everything to gain from being sensitive and careful. Who knows what is happening in your partner's life that is causing him to fall down on the job? Approaching the conversation with patience and honesty can only work in your favor. Consider the following pointers.

◆ Choose a time when you are alone and can easily talk. Don't pull him aside in a busy hallway at school, or start questioning him, no matter how quietly, at the lunch table. He is probably well aware that he has not been working as hard as you. If he thinks others are listening he's bound to become very embarrassed and even more defensive than he might ordinarily.

◆ Begin by asking him if he's having some sort of problem. Tell him he's seemed a little absentminded lately (which is very likely true) and that you couldn't help thinking something was up.

◆ If he admits that something is wrong, you should be as sympathetic as you can. Then you will have to mention your own concerns. "I'm sorry that's happening, but I'm also worried about this project. I think you need some help, but so do we!" If he insists nothing is wrong, you will have to straightforwardly explain the major reason you were asking.

◆ Phrase everything you feel in terms of "I feel . . ." and "It seems to me . . ." instead of "You never . . ." or "You don't . . ." This communicates the idea that you are open to changing your views. It is also difficult to argue with. If you *feel* a particular way, your partner can't say, "No you don't!"

◆ Point out exactly what you have been doing. Concentrate on the amount of work you have contributed—not on what he hasn't done.

◆ Matter-of-factly tell him exactly what it is you would like him to do. There's no point complaining about what he hasn't done. But there's a lot to be gained in being crystal clear about what you would like to have happen now.

◆ Make sure he realizes how much you know he could contribute. Let him know that you are sorely missing his participation, not just because you feel as if you've been doing most of the work, but also because you think he could contribute things you cannot. People like to feel needed.

If your partner argues that you are wrong, insisting that he's done plenty, give it a couple of days. He may be a person who can't face up to his behavior, even though he

knows he's wrong. Watch what he does. He may very well begin to work harder.

However, if his behavior doesn't change, or if in fact he does have a problem that is making it difficult for him to work, your teacher should be consulted. You should do so if he simply refuses to participate fully, or he should do so if he's suffering with a problem that is affecting his work. If he does tell the teacher he's too distressed to do his part, you will have to speak to the teacher as well. Either you will need a new partner or the assignment will have to be altered to reflect that only one person is doing the work.

And of course you should each be clear with each other about how you intend to proceed. If your partner doesn't recognize his problem, you should tell him you're going to speak to the teacher. If he intends to speak to the teacher, you should ask that he let you know so that you can enlist her aid in either finding you another partner or adjusting your work load.

The bottom line is that you should not be left to shoulder alone the entire burden of a project meant for two. Suffering silently is no answer. You'll likely become very angry, and your project will suffer.

Partnerships can be very rewarding. But they can be terribly frustrating and disappointing, too. Often they simply need a jump start. A serious, honest discussion can sometimes light a wonderful fire of productivity. But other times nothing will spark that flame.

Just as partnerships are formed, so do they dissolve. Yours won't be the first and it won't be the last. You just have to move on and get whatever project you end up with done!

Getting along

Q You have just been assigned a partner with whom you have to make a geography presentation. The problem is, you don't like her. She's very serious and kind of out-of-it. In fact, you don't think she likes you, either.

A It's nice to be able to work with a friend, but it can't always happen. Many times in school and in the workplace you will find yourself working with a person with whom you would not be talking were it not for the task at hand.

But that's okay.

Whether or not your personalities mesh, or whether or not you think she's funny or interesting or sensitive, simply should not matter. What does matter is whether or not this person does her job.

Does she do her part of the assignment in a timely fashion?

Does she contribute something to the assignment that you could not?

Is she helpful to you as you complete your part?

Does she give and take criticism well?

When it comes to getting a job done, how we feel about a partner often doesn't matter as much as our ability to work together. You don't have to like someone personally to work with her. You do, however, have to respect her and feel that she respects you.

You may not enjoy your partner's personality, but that doesn't mean you can't allow her to contribute her skills to the project.

You may not like her jokes, but that doesn't mean she wouldn't be good at catching a flaw in her or your work.

You may not have anything in common, but that doesn't mean you can't discuss any potential pitfalls in the project you are designing together.

You are not working together to become friends; you are working together to complete an assignment. If you can keep this in mind, you should get through the project just fine.

As a matter of fact, you might get through the project with more ease than you would have with a good friend. Sometimes friends as partners are so worried about hurting each other's feelings or being accused of insensitivity or a whole host of other things that the project falls completely apart!

In other words, it can actually be easier to get a job done when you're working with someone with whom your relationship is not a priority. It's easier to say, "No! I don't think that will work," and to hear her snap back, "Oh, stop being so negative!" when the two of you are not risking a friendship.

The one exception to this is if you are working with

HELP!

My project partner is kind of the class doof. People are going to be laughing at me.

Chances are, you feel worried because you don't want to be rejected. You don't want people thinking you're weird because you have to work with this person. But they won't. Not unless, of course, *you* think you're weird.

The truth is, the way you view yourself will have the greatest effect on how others view you. If you think you're hip, chances are they will, too. If you don't, they may suspect you aren't. Which brings us to this "weird" partner. It may be tempting to blow him off so that your friends know you consider him a geek. But that would be cruel and a little cowardly. Instead, treat him well no matter who is around and act like the decent person you are. Your friends might tease you, but deep down they'll think you're pretty brave. They may even decide this guy isn't so weird after all.

But don't count on it. Your friends may need to have a "doof" in their midst in order to feel good about themselves.

someone who is bossy, un-helpful, critical, and given to laughing at your every mis-take. That is unacceptable.

If this happens to you, im-mediately tell your partner that she has to stop. Plain and simple. "We're partners in this project. I'm not making fun of you and I'm not bossing you around. Don't do it to me."

Chances are, if you con-front her directly, she'll stop. If she doesn't, you have two choices. One, you can tell your teacher that the situation has become unbearable, in which case she might suggest you divide up the project in such a way that your contact is minimal, or she might call a meeting with the two of you

and try to straighten things out. Your second choice is to ignore your partner's obnox-ious behavior, get through the project, and call it a day.

Sometimes just saying to yourself, "You know, this per-son doesn't matter. What mat-ters is getting this job done. Then I never have to speak to her again," can be very helpful.

This realization is proba-bly one of the more important lessons of your collaboration. The work is the easy part. The working relationship is the tough part. Your teachers know this, and it is one reason they create cooperative learn-ing assignments. Teamwork is a skill you will need through-out life.

Late with assignments

Q Your book report is due tomorrow. The assignment was given last week, but you kept putting it off, thinking you'd get to it later. You didn't. And now there is no way you're going to hand it in on time.

A You have a lot to organize in your life. You have lots of different classes and lots of different assignments. Your friends want your time, your parents expect you to do your chores, you have your outside interests, and then, of course, you want to have time to just hang out and do nothing.

The trouble is, there are only twenty-four hours in a day. Usually something has to give. The trick is for you to control which thing that is.

You need to become more organized. This is not an easy thing to do. It takes many students quite awhile to get used to the concept of planning ahead. But they do it, because it's the only way to make sure everything gets done. You can't just do a little here, a little there, and then hope by the time the clock stops ticking all will be completed. That's

HELP!

My English teacher keeps giving out homework as if hers is the only homework we have! I can't fit it all in and neither can my friends in the class!

Tell her. Take a friend or two with you along with lots of facts. Show her the day's homework assignments. If necessary, let her see how much work went into last night's math and history homework. Be calm and organized. Also, bring a suggestion as to how to change the assignment, so your teacher understands you're not trying to avoid doing the work altogether. Chances are, your teacher will either adjust the assignment right then and there, or at least agree to talk to your other teachers in order to reach some sort of compromise. (She won't want to be the only teacher cutting back on assignments.) If neither of these things happens, organize a few people to speak to a counselor at school. He or she will probably schedule a group meeting of your class teachers to resolve the problem.

magic. That's not life.

It's critical that you look at the week ahead, figure out about how long it will take you to do your assignments, and then block out the time to do the work. Then you have to be strict with yourself. If someone calls while you're working and says, "Hey! Let's go to the mall," you have to say, "I can't right now." (Remember to say "right now" both to your friend and yourself. It makes a nice reminder that you won't always have to say no.)

As for what you tell your teacher, honesty is best. "I thought I'd have enough time to do it, but I messed up. I'm sorry. I'll get it to you by tomorrow."

Your teacher may or may not respond in a positive manner. A lot will depend on your record to date (do you generally hand in assignments on time?), and also the sort of approach she takes. If she's a "go by the rules" type, she may tell you that she will have to lower your grade on the re-

port. If she is more flexible, she might simply comment that she hopes you've learned a lesson, and that this will not be acceptable if it happens again.

The most important thing to take away from this experience, no matter what your teacher says or does, is that planning is of paramount importance. So the next time you get an assignment, don't just shove it in the back of your notebook because it's not due for a week and that's seven whole days away! A week goes by very quickly. Figure out how much time the assignment will take and then look at your schedule. Decide when you will do the work, and then keep to your plan. You may block out an entire afternoon for an assignment, or you may choose to spread it out an hour a day for three days. It doesn't

matter. What matters is that you give yourself the time to do the job right.

And if something has to suffer because of your limited time, you be the one to decide which thing it will be. That's part of the plan, too. If you have to tell a coach you've got a tough assignment to complete, do it. If you have to skip Guitar Club, let the members know. If you can't handle all your chores, let your parents know before they are due to get done.

You know what's most important. Just stay on top of it. And if you don't know, consult with a counselor at school. He or she will help you clarify what issues need the most attention, and how to work out a realistic schedule.

Family attention

Chapter 6

Most parents have lots of expectations when it comes to their child's school performance, and most kids resent every last one of them.

Sometimes these expectations are high in every way. Other times they are more flexible and relaxed. Most often they are somewhere in between.

But whatever these expectations are, they have a way of seeming very unfair, as if they have been designed for one student, while you are quite definitely another.

And maybe they are un-

fair—that's possible, too.

But before we get into that, let's look at this issue of your parents' interest in your work from another perspective. Let's look at what's right and fair about it.

Your parents expect you to do your best. Even if your

best is not what they'd have liked, this expectation is a fair one. The truth is, school is your "job." It's your responsibility. And it is also an important part of your future. If you do well in school, you will likely go on to a good college. If you do well in college, you will likely go on to a graduate degree and/or a rewarding career. People who do their best, who work hard, who give themselves over to the job at hand, are usually the people who succeed in life. (This is so whether or not college is in the picture.) There's a lot of competition out there! You've got to bring your whole self to an undertaking.

Your parents want you to be prepared. This is why they expect you to work extra-hard to strengthen a weak area, and not to simply do well with what comes easily. Many times in life you will come up against a difficult assignment. Perhaps it will be an aspect of your job. You might be called upon to write a report when in fact you're better at statistical analysis. What are you going to say to your boss: "Sorry. That's not my strength"? Of course not! You're going to work very hard at making that report as good as it can be. This ability to buckle down and go that extra mile to hand in good work is a necessary skill that begins in school.

Your parents might sometimes say they expect you to do as well as they "know you can." Putting aside whether or not they are right about what you can and can't do, consider the possibility that you aren't right, either. Their assumptions about your academic strengths might actually be more accurate than you think! Your study habits might be holding you back. Your social life might be taking up too much time. Feelings of insecurity might be negatively affecting your work. But also, imagine this possibility: You might be more able than you think, and by seeing the compliment in what your parents are saying, you will discover you can do better.

Of course, your parents are only human, and therefore, imperfect. Keep in mind that they have problems and issues, too, that may impact unfairly on the way they see things. Your parents may be hoping to relive their own successes through you. They may be striving to ensure that you won't make the same mistakes or exhibit the same weakness they did. They may be trying to prove their own worth as parents through your academic successes. Finally, they may simply be people who have always set very tough goals for themselves, and thus take the same approach with you. The trouble is, these "issues" ignore one very important thing.

And that's *you*.

In worrying about correcting the past, or seeing themselves as good parents, or making sure you approach life the way they do, your parents may sometimes forget to see you as a separate, often very different person from themselves.

In fact, when they get upset with you, it's important to realize that sometimes it's not just you in whom they are disappointed and upset. It's also themselves. Maybe you got a particular weakness from them. Maybe they did something which has caused you not to respect or admire them. Perhaps that's why you don't follow their advice.

Finally, there is another kind of parent. These are the ones who are so busy, or struggling with a problem so large, they don't seem to notice what you are doing. They are consumed by the difficulties they are having, and you seem to be getting lost in the shuffle. If this is your circumstance, it's especially important for you to take to heart the core message of this book. Your education is up to you. The most available or involved parent cannot make a student do his or her best. The real motivation to do well has to come from within. While you may not have your parents' attention, you do still have *you*.

And that is what will make the real difference.

The bottom line is, you can't expect your parents to just step away from what you do at school. Most of them will think it's too important for that. But you can and should expect that their in-volvement be a balanced and constructive one.

The first step is finding a way to communicate when what happens at school doesn't meet with expectations from home. This chapter will help you do just that—and then some.

Parents vs. friends

Q You've begun hanging out with a fast crowd at school. Your parents and teachers feel these kids are a bad influence on you and are strongly suggesting you not see them anymore. You are very angry at their attempts to control your life.

A Put aside for a moment what your parents or teachers think. It matters, but something else matters even more: What do *you* think?

Before you do or say anything, it's very important to run a reality test for yourself. You need to try and see the facts as clearly as you can. Why do your parents feel these friends are a bad influence? Are your grades slipping? Are you getting into fights with people? Are you disruptive in class? What are the facts?

If none of these things are happening, and you think it's a case of your parents being too strict, or not understanding your friends, or believing that you can't make good choices for yourself, then feel annoyed ... but stay calm. Getting angry won't help. It will only make you look out of control, which is precisely what your parents are afraid of. They are anxious that you will come under the influence of this crowd and lose your sense of priorities, of what's right and wrong.

You need to sit down with your parents and listen to exactly what it is they are afraid of. Do they think these friends drink or take drugs? Are they worried that you're being pressured to take risks, test boundaries, or just plain goof off? If none of these things are true, then say so. Give them examples. Prove your point.

Parents are people, too. They love you more than anything, and because of that love they tend to see danger where there may not be any. They may not know your friends very well, and are thus unaware of their positive but less visible sides. Try and understand that when talking with them. It should help you feel less offended and annoyed, and more able to defend your choices.

However, what if your reality test proves that though you hadn't connected the two, your grades have been slipping and you are getting into trouble? The smartest thing you can do is own up to it. Promise yourself and then your parents that you will straighten out. Take whatever steps necessary to do so. This does not have to include leaving the crowd, especially if they are flexible and ready to accept you the way you want to be.

Straightening up will probably require that you spend less time with them. It may even demand that you avoid going certain places, or playing along with some "adventures." But if they're solid friends, and truly offer you things other than a chance to walk on the wild side, they'll understand you have to do what you have to do.

Once your grades and behavior record improve, your parents and teachers are likely to relax considerably. You'll have shown them you can be trusted and relied upon to make mature and honest judgment calls.

Of course, you may not be at all interested in considering anything. You might just feel, upon hearing your parents' and teachers' requests, that you are sick and tired of being told what to do. You're not a baby, you might tell yourself, and no matter what others think, or even what's true, you will do as you like.

Well, that's true. You will do as you like. Your parents are unlikely to put you in a cage. Your teachers certainly

can't. But you do have to keep in mind that you are responsible for your own decisions. You are also the one who has to pay the price, if there is one, for whatever it is you decide. In other words, if you are going to take the position that you will do as you please, it would be smart to make sure what you're doing is worth it. Don't get seduced by the rebellious notion of doing what you want "no matter what anyone thinks" or by the glitter of things forbidden. There's a saying, "Stolen sweets are sweeter," which when translated into practical terms means forbidden things always seem more attractive. But that's no excuse to take risks, because in truth those sweets aren't sweeter. In fact, they could be downright bitter. If what you're after is some sense of independence, then consider this. You can prove you are your own boss by choosing to do things that aren't self-destructive, just as well as by choosing things that may be.

HELP!

My parents don't want me to see this kid I really like, so I have to sneak time with him. It feels bad.

The question you have to ask yourself is, why does it feel bad? Have you considered your parents' reasons carefully? If you haven't, you might wonder if the bad feelings come from your suspicions that they are right and you should keep away. On the other hand, if you have thought about their fears and honestly feel they are ill-founded, then you probably just feel bad because you are behaving in a dishonest way.

So then the question becomes, is sneaking worth the bad feeling? That will depend on how much you care about this kid, and how convinced you are that your parents are wrong. While disobeying your parents is not a good thing, to simply do as they say when you strongly feel it is not right will only bring you pain and eat away at your relationship with them.

One suggestion: You might, after a short period of time, tell your parents something nice about this friend and suggest that maybe he could come to your house for a visit when they are home. That way they could see for themselves that he may not be as bad an influence as they think. In other words, if you choose to continue sneaking in time to see him, be sure to keep working on changing the atmosphere at home so that you no longer have to sneak.

The bottom line is, people who are concerned for you will step in and comment about choices you make throughout your life. You may not like their tone. You may not have invited a single remark. But you might want to listen. They may have a perspective that is both useful and informative. Ultimately, what you do is up to you. But choosing to act one way just to prove you don't have to listen to anyone is silly.

Buckling under immediately to what others think you should do is silly, too. Ultimately, the wisest choices come from listening to everyone (or at least those you respect), being as honest as you can, and then acting in accordance with what you truly think is right for you. That way, if you're right you can feel wonderful, and if you're wrong you can at least know you did the best you could.

Report card jitters

Q You've just received a bad report card. You feel terrible about it. But the anticipation of facing your parents feels worse. In fact, you're actually afraid to show them the report card. You can just imagine the disappointment and anger you're going to have to face.

A While talking to your parents might be uppermost on your mind, there is no point facing them with your disappointing grades until you've sorted out how it happened and what you're going to do about it.

Chances are, this report card is no surprise. Still, you might have been pushing the facts (and lousy grades) out of your mind hoping they'd just magically kind of mutate into more favorable letters. Your parents are likely to have lots of questions, and you will want to have mature answers that reflect your own concern.

Have you been goofing

HELP!

My mother volunteers for everything at school. It drives me crazy! Class trips. Chaperoning dances. Bake sales. My friends are constantly teasing me!

Tell her. But do it nicely. Your mother probably needs to be a presence at your school for many reasons. Perhaps she wants to be close to you, perhaps she wants to have some constructive influence over what happens there, and perhaps it just plain makes her feel useful. You can't take her needs away. But you may be able to help her redirect them. "Mom, I really appreciate how much you like helping my class out, but to be honest the kids are teasing me because you're around so much. Do you think you could do something a little more behind-the-scenes and let someone else's parent be at the dance? It's hard for me when you're at every event. I need to feel that I'm on my own more at these things."

Chances are, your mother will hear you. If not, you might also try speaking to your teacher, who could gently suggest to your mother—when she volunteers for yet another activity—that he already has enough parents to help out . . . but thank you.

off, and if so, are you prepared to do something about it now? Are some subjects difficult for you this year? What can you do to improve things? Can your parents help in any way? Is there an emotional problem you are wrestling with that is getting in the way of your concentration? Do you need some help sorting it out? Is there a teacher with whom you can't get along? Do you feel at least one of your grades is a reflection of this problem?

Try and be as honest with yourself as you can. One grade may indicate a particular problem between you and a teacher or subject, but an overall disappointing report card usually has more to do with things that are going on inside of you, rather than outside forces. Making claims such as, "I did everything. I studied real hard. My teachers are awful," may only work during the conversation with your parents. As soon as they check in with your school, they will likely find out the truth about your slacking off.

If you *have* slacked off, figure out why. Then explain what has gone on to your parents. If it appears that you are taking mature responsibility for your actions, they will probably trust that your grades will improve. Of course, depending on their attitudes and beliefs, they may still be anything from furious to mildly annoyed to obviously disappointed. But no matter what your parents' reaction is, it will not be the most important thing.

In the long run, what matters is your attitude toward your work. Your parents will get over their annoyance, and a marked improvement in your grades will undo the damage to your record. The question is, do you now have a clearer idea of what you want to accomplish and the best way to get there? Different people will expect you to "deliver" in different ways throughout your life. But the most important person of all, the person you need to answer to, is you.

Parental expectations

Q You are a very conscientious student and your grades are usually excellent. But you've just gotten back a geometry test and instead of your usual A, you got a B. You're afraid to show it to your parents. They expect you to receive top grades in everything. They'll think you shouldn't have gone out this weekend (even though it was just a short time), and maybe they're right.

A You are a human being with lots of needs. You have every right to want to enjoy yourself socially. There are just so many hours in the day, and something has to give to accommodate different aspects of your life. This may mean taking a little time away from a rigorous studying schedule.

Also, just because you took some time to socialize, that's not necessarily the reason you got a B. No one is perfect. Geometry can be complicated and you might have had a difficult time with the test anyway.

In terms of your parents expecting perfect grades, are

you absolutely sure about this? Perhaps you too expect perfection? Sometimes we can feel things so intensely that we assume others feel them, too. It's possible that you are your own harshest judge. Certainly you should take a responsible attitude toward your work. Parties are no excuse for poor grades. But you can't expect yourself to do fabulously in school every step of the way. That's what learning is about. It's about strengthening your skills. It's about gaining knowledge. And it's about learning to think in new ways. The process practically requires that you struggle through some work!

Assuming, however, that your parents *are* very demanding, you should first hear them out. Are they critical of the way you are spending your time? If so, try explaining how you feel about your social life and point out that overall your grades are still terrific. Volunteer to get a little extra help with your geometry, and assure them that you care about

your work. Do they suspect you're going to start taking your work less seriously? Let them know this isn't so by clearly and calmly pointing out your other grades and explaining why you had a problem on this test.

Most important, gently remind them that you just can't be perfect and you'd like it a lot if they didn't ask that of you. "I wish I could do everything just right, too. But I can't. I have to learn stuff, too. Please give me a little room to fall down sometimes."

If it feels as if you are not getting through, suggest a meeting between you, your teacher, and your parents to help open up the lines of communication between you.

Whatever you do, don't sit on your hurt, anger, or resentful feelings toward your parents. Some students become so upset by high-pressure parents that they "close down shop." They rebel by refusing to work and allowing all their grades to plummet. "I'll show them," they think, forgetting to focus on the fact that they are hurting themselves as well.

Rebelling can be an easy trap to fall into, because sorting out problems with parents can be painful and very hard work. But keep at it. If you need help, speak to the counselor at school for some moral support. And do allow yourself time to enjoy every aspect of your life.

When it comes to study-ing, it's not just the quantity of time spent working that matters, it's also the quality. Chances are, if all you did was work, your mind would begin wandering to the places and people you wish you were seeing. But if you allowed yourself to socialize, most likely when you did study, you'd concentrate.

It's a question of balance, which isn't easy. But it is possible.

Successful sibling

Q Your older brother was a fabulous student. You are not. Instead, your greatest strengths lie in the arts; music to be exact. Your parents can't seem to accept this. Repeatedly they remind you of your brother's success, your own intelligence, and their concern about why you're not repeating your brother's performance.

First and foremost, you have to give yourself permission not to be your brother. This does not mean, of course, that you should allow yourself to do poorly! But it does mean that before you can explain to someone who you're not, you have to believe in who you are.

You also need to consider exactly who is putting the pressure on you. Your parents may indeed occasionally comment, perhaps insensitively, about your school record as compared to your brother's, but do you do that as well? Your own feeling of competition might be so intense that you are beginning to believe that everyone in the world is comparing the two of you all of the time.

It's possible and natural that you might feel disappointed that your grades are not as good as your brother's were. You might wonder if you're less intelligent, or whether the teachers talk about you, or whether you will ever measure up to him.

As a result, any comment from your parents might seem twice as hurtful than it might if you felt surer of yourself.

The question is, how can you feel more confident when there's a "legend" in your home? First, make a list of your special strengths. And not just your schoolwork pluses, either. Are you a supportive friend? Do you have a quick sense of humor? Consider everything about you that you know is solid. Be sure and include items that your brother and you share as well as strengths that are yours alone. (If the list you come up with seems woefully slim, remember this. Strengths and interests develop over time. Talents are often discovered later in life. Some famous painters began their careers in their fifties!)

Then have a frank talk with your brother. Tell him how difficult it is for you to live up to his record. Ask him if he was always sure of himself. You might be very surprised at what you hear. He might tell you that he's always envied certain aspects of who you are! And most surprisingly, he might even tell you that your parents have often thrown you up in his face! "Your younger brother loves playing the flute," they might have said. "Why aren't you interested in music?"

Which gets us to the issue of parents who compare their children. The truth is, it's a useless and hurtful thing to do. Everyone is different. Everyone has his own strengths and weaknesses. Family genes don't necessarily make similar people. But parents sometimes forget this. Something wonderful appears in one child, and so they expect to see it in the others. It's a pride thing. "Look what we made," they think. In the process they often fail to respect the special things that emerge in their other children.

Another reason parents may compare children is to motivate them. They may think that pointing out a sibling's talents will inspire you.

Give you confidence. They may think it will make it extremely clear that you too can be as good at a certain thing. Which of course may not be true. Or they might choose to compare in order to get the competitive juices flowing. Perhaps they think it will motivate you to work harder and prove yourself.

But whether it's pride, or a desire to build confidence, or the sense that competition will do the trick, parents usually hurt their children when they start making comparisons. And the only way for them to find this out is if you tell them. Clearly.

So write them a letter. Describe how hurt or angry you feel when they compare the two of you. Point out your special strengths. Tell them how you deserve to be appreciated for who you are. Write down everything and anything you feel. Allow it to clarify your feelings. Then read the letter over a few times. This will make you feel a lot better.

Then tear it up.

The above technique is called venting. You get everything out, just the way you want to say it, without worrying at all about anyone else's reaction. You express the anger, the frustration, the sorrow, without focusing at all on anyone else's thoughts and feelings. It can feel wonderful. Venting out loud, however, won't. Nor will it be informative for your parents who will be too busy defending themselves to listen. Any important conversation between people, especially when it comes to highly emotional subjects, needs to be handled carefully. The best results come from talks in which each person respects not just what he or she is feeling, but also what the other person is feeling, too.

Finally, sit down with your parents and tell them, *calmly,* how you feel. As stated in this book before, feelings cannot be contradicted. A person can't say, "You don't feel that way!" Also, your parents will not experience your words as an attack, which is a very important thing to keep in mind.

◆ "I feel that I work hard. My teachers think so, too."
◆ "I love music. It's so interesting to me. I like my other subjects, too, but I don't feel as easy with them. I'm trying, though."
◆ "I'm good at many things my brother never even tried. I feel like you don't appreciate that."
◆ "I feel hurt when you compare me to my brother. I think we're very different people, and I feel as if you're telling me I'm less good."
◆ "I'm just not as good as my brother at math. I try. I feel awful when you compare us."

The point is to stay away from such accusations as "You

always make me feel terrible" or "You only care about the things I can't do well. You don't care about me" or "You're so unfair and mean." People who have to defend their actions don't have time to hear everything that is being

HELP!

I knew my grades were slipping! I just somehow forgot about it until my report card came, and then it was too late!

This is called "denial," which is when a person knows something but, because it's too hard to face, pretends he doesn't know it and pushes the thought away. Or convinces himself that it will change, while doing nothing to change it. Why? Because it's easier. You probably became upset by your poor grades but were afraid of the work it would take to fix them, and also of the possibility that maybe you couldn't do better even if you tried. And so you did nothing. But as you can see, that doesn't work. Denying something doesn't make it go away. There's no big mystery to this situation. You have to face that you let things slide and take action. You can't just hope or dream or push it away. You have to *do something*. And then you have to keep your expectations reasonable. If you have a lot of work to catch up, things may improve slowly. Don't let it discourage you. It's the only option you've got to turn things around. You can't deny that!

said. If your parents have to defend what they've said to you, they may not hear how you feel about it. And that's the part they need to focus upon.

One final note about comparisons that you should remember when comparing yourself to someone else. Comparisons can be very dangerous. There will always be someone smarter than you, or more talented, or more handsome, or more athletic. But there will never be another person just like you. Your particular traits all come together to form a unique person. If you don't respect the things about you that make you special, other people will have a difficult time doing so, too.

But parents should know better, you might say to yourself. And you're right, they should. In fact, many do. But does that mean those parents are better than the ones who slip up and compare siblings? Probably not. Probably the parents who don't compare make mistakes your parents wouldn't. Every parent is different.

Sound familiar?

Problems at home

Q You are having some major problems at home. Your parents are fighting constantly and the tension in the house is awful. It's getting harder and harder to concentrate on your work, and unfortunately it shows. Your grades are slipping, making you feel even worse. But most of all you're feeling very lonely.

A The most important thing you can do in a situation like this is give yourself a break. People can't just leave their problems behind when it's not a good time to think about them. There's an old saying that goes, "A traveler takes himself with him." You can move around all you want, but you will bring the essence of who you are, *and* your problems, wherever you go. That's not bad. It's just a fact.

Divorce, financial reverses, sickness, and death are only a few of the serious problems families deal with all of the time. These difficult issues weigh heavily on all family members, wherever they are. You happen to be in school most of the time, so that is where you bring your problems. It is also where you probably work very hard not to let them show. This can make a person very lonely.

It can be hard to talk about very personal, serious problems. You might opt not to discuss them, in an effort to deny to yourself and others that they exist. Or you might decide not to discuss them because it may seem to you that none of your friends would understand. It might appear they are living happy-go-lucky lives and wouldn't be able to understand your problems at all.

But this may not be true.

Many kids who are confused or upset by problems at home keep them to themselves. Just like you. They somehow feel embarrassed to admit their parents aren't getting along, or that their mother or father lost a job, or even that a relative is seriously sick. What if someone laughs or says the wrong thing? What if someone makes them feel even more alone than they already do?

But the thing is, what if you and a friend could actually help each other?

Sharing a problem with a person who really cares for you could do many things. It could give you a new perspective on the problem you are having. It could enlighten you about the things that happen in other people's lives. (There's a funny thing about telling someone about a problem. They often share one of their own!) Knowing you are not the only one with difficulties can sometimes make you feel less isolated. And finally, sharing problems brings people closer. While you may feel as if you are losing ground at home in terms of feeling safe and secure, you may actually gain back some confidence from being honest with your friends.

Wait until you have some private time with a friend, and then just take the plunge. "You know, I'm having this problem I really need to talk about . . ." is a perfectly fine beginning, as is "Do you mind if I tell you something really personal that's upsetting me? I think I'd feel better if I could talk about it . . ."

As for your grades, certainly you will want to reverse this downward spiral. Opening up to friends should help to make you feel steadier and less alone. They might offer to give you some academic help. As a result your grades might start improving. But chances are you will need to confide in either a school counselor or a teacher so that you will gain their understanding and patience, and so that they can

help you catch up on your work in a helpful, supportive manner.

Talk to them. That's what they're there for. No matter what you tell them about your family life, they will not seek to blame it on you. They will only feel sorry that you have been under such stress. They are adults. They've lived long enough to know that difficult things happen to good people. They know that grown-ups have trouble coping, and that kids, who have much less experience with adversity, have an even tougher time.

And finally, keep this in mind. While sagging grades are a drag, what counts most of all is how you *feel*. It is critical to your mental health that you pay attention to your emotions. Depression, anger, and sorrow are only a few of the difficult feelings with which we all sometimes need help. If you go out and get the

H E L P !

I'm scared. I think my friend is being abused at home, but he isn't talking.

If you suspect that there is some abuse going on, whether you are right or wrong, you owe it to your friend, yourself, and your friendship to try and get at the truth. It can feel like an awesome responsibility, and one that you might wish you could push away, but you can't. Part of being a caring human being is valuing the safety and health of others.

First, try and get your friend to open up. Wait for him to bring up something that happened at home, or for a moment when you are alone and he's letting his sadness show. Then, ask your questions, but do so with a gentle hand. If he is being abused, he may feel a responsibility to protect that parent because, despite the pain, he loves him or her. Also, your friend may

be very mixed-up and fear that somehow he's to blame. Understand that you are walking into very sensitive territory and so you'll have to be delicate.

◆ If your friend has just told you part of a story and you suspect there's more, try, "Wow. That must have upset you a lot. It would have upset me. Did anything else happen after that?" By offering sympathy and the notion that you too would feel a certain way, your friend may feel more confident about revealing the truth.

◆ If your friend is merely looking sad and you sense he wants to tell you something, you might try, "You know, I know things are rough at your house. Are you okay? You look like you feel real bad, and maybe if I listened it could help." Saying you want to hear him is a very tempting invitation, even more so than inviting him to "talk." You're making it clear that you want to take in what he's saying without making a judgment.

◆ If your friend has told you a few things but has done so with a chuckle as if it's no big deal, but you are really worried, tell him so. Let him see that you think what's happening to him isn't fair. He may need that perspective in order to allow himself to confront a painful truth. If he is being abused, it has to stop.

Of course, there are no guarantees that your friend will admit a thing. At the conclusion of your attempts you may still have nothing more than your suspicions. However, your friend,

after a while, may reveal some pretty awful things. He may describe emotional, physical, or sexual abuse. He may also beg you not to repeat anything he is telling you. He may fear getting his parent in trouble. He may fear even worse abuse at home if it becomes clear that he has told. He may also threaten you with the friendship, saying that if you repeat a word he'll never talk to you again.

At this point you will probably wish you didn't know or suspect a thing. But you do. And you have to act. Abuse is simply not tolerable. Neither is ignoring it.

It's important for you to talk to the school counselor or psychologist about your fears. You just have to be as clear as you can about what you know as opposed to what you suspect so that

(continued on next page)

aid and support you need, you will feel better. Once that happens, your grades will more than likely improve.

Note: Sometimes prob-

lems at home are even more serious than an impending divorce or a sick relative. If you or a member of your family is being hurt or abused in any

(continued from previous page)
things can be handled in a careful, reasonable manner. Your object is not to prove that you are right. Rather, it's to get your suspicions checked out. The counselor will want to speak to your friend as soon as possible and may ask if you think you could help bring him to the office. This is up to you. The counselor will find a way to see him. Once you report this sort of suspicion the counselor is required to look into the situation. He will begin by talking to your friend.

If you feel you need some support, speak to your parents before revealing what you know to anyone at school. But as soon as you

are able, with or without your parents, tell the school counselor or psychologist what you have heard. Be sure and mention your friend's fears of further abuse. Your school counselor will contact professionals at a protective service agency who are trained to assess and handle these specific kinds of circumstances and to help all of the people involved. Your friend is not the only person in pain. His parents need help, too.

Which brings us to a difficult reality. Even though your friend may be treated unkindly at home, what is happening may fall short of what officials call abuse. In some cases there is

way, it is especially important that you speak to a school counselor rather than a teacher who is not trained to handle certain kinds of painful and delicate problems. (If what you have to report is tremendously serious, a teacher may not respond in a manner that is helpful. His own distress over

very little that can be done, though school officials will certainly watch the student carefully for any signs of more serious problems. In other cases the family will probably be monitored for a period of time by the agency and may even be required to get some therapy to alleviate the problem.

As for risking your friendship, you have to look at the situation with a clear head. Sure, you want to stay buddies, but how can you do that knowing that your friend is in trouble and that you are doing nothing? Your silence will begin to cause you pain, and will in effect allow your friend's to continue. That's not a healthy friendship. So in a way you

have no choice. And if at first your friend is angry that you repeated what he's said, it won't matter if in the end he ends up safer and better for it. Hopefully he'll thank you. But if he doesn't, if because of his mixed-up feelings he stays angry, at least you'll know you protected a friend. That should give you a terrific feeling.

Note: If you are uncomfortable relating your suspicions to the school, or if you want to remain anonymous, call 911 and request a hotline number for reporting suspected child abuse. You can phone in your concerns without stating your name. The family will be checked out.

your story could get in the way.) Whether or not you choose to discuss this with your friends is up to you, but whether or not you say anything to the authorities shouldn't be. Abuse, be it emotional, physical, or sexual, has to be reported. There are people out there who know how to handle families who are in trouble in a sensitive, effective manner. You will not be blamed or punished for speaking out.

Chapter 7

Sports spots

Sports, you probably figure, ought to be fun. It's a chance to cut loose, to just get out there and let your body feel good. It's your time to work out those frustrations or disappointments you've had in the classroom. You can take that competitive streak you like to hide and bring it right out in the open!

At many times, this is exactly how participating in school sports will feel.

But it's unrealistic to expect that school sports will give you nothing but a fun outlet for your pent-up energy, emotions, and talent. The truth is, organized sports require much of the same kinds of discipline that the classroom demands. You need the same awareness of your own strengths and weaknesses, and the same willingness to work and follow the rules. In most sports, either in practice or during a game or competition, you need to function as part of a team, much as you do as a member of a class. In fact, unlike in the classroom, there's often an added pressure. What you do can profoundly affect the rest of the team. And always, you must perform under the watchful eye of an authority figure.

As a result, you may actually feel, while participating in a school-organized sport, that sometimes it's not that much fun. Practice may seem like a bore, your coach's expectations may seem completely out of line, and your love of the sport may feel compromised by a grueling schedule and your occasional inability to perform as well as you would like. You might feel tired, embarrassed, unappreciated, or ignored.

This will likely catapult you into a confusing dilemma that is the single biggest difference between school sports and schoolwork: With sports, you can opt to say no.

You can decide that organized sports at your school—this particular year, with this

particular coach, considering the particular way you feel—just doesn't feel right. There is, after all, usually a very satisfactory alternative. You can organize games with friends. Or, if your sport is a solitary one, you can enjoy it when you are able to fit it in. For many students, this is without a doubt the best way to go.

Of course, deciding to leave a team is not easy. Donning that official uniform, hearing the cheers of the home crowd, and knowing you and your teammates have a joint goal combine to create an extraordinary experience.

If you don't want to, you shouldn't. But in order to stick it out you may need to alter your expectations and remember that organized sports will always have its difficult moments.

In fact, informal games can be tough, too.

Let's face it. If you strike out, it doesn't matter where you're playing, or against whom. It isn't going to feel terrific.

Endless drills

Q Last month you made it onto the varsity basketball team. You were thrilled. The trouble is, now you can barely stand to attend practice. You want to get out there and play, but all the coach wants to do is drill, drill, drill.

A Coaches, just like teachers, come in different packages. Some will be everything you ever wanted in a coach and some won't. Each will approach the task at hand with a different set of priorities.

One coach may be a very conservative type of person. He or she may insist on drill after drill, believing that you have to get the basic moves completely down before a proper, well-executed game can be played.

Another coach might think the mixed approach is best. Some drills, together with a spirited game, will afford your team the best experience and strongest skills.

Then there are those coaches who view the team as a fine machine, with each player being an important component. They want no flashy moves, no independent

thinking. Everyone has to work together. Other coaches might encourage each player to take advantage of his or her own gifts and to take chances accordingly.

What it gets down to is that most kids join a team because they enjoy the sport and like the competitive feeling. These are excellent reasons for signing on. But while your coach is there to guide you toward a strong game, the path to this goal can take many different directions.

If you are unhappy with the way your coach is handling the team, you have two choices. One, you can opt to speak with him privately about the way you think things are going. If you don't like the constant drilling, you might ask if he could set aside a small amount of time for a practice game. If you feel you've been asked to sit on your special skills, you might ask if there's some extra practice you could put in to inspire him to allow you to use your "stuff" more. In other words,

you *can* absolutely ask for whatever it is you think you're missing from this much-sought-after experience.

However, you can't expect things to change. The truth is, your coach may have very strong ideas about how to best do his job, and may be unwilling to change them. The school administration, too, might be putting pressure on him. Perhaps your school has a reputation for having a fine basketball team. He doesn't want to be the one under whom the team falters. Also, he may not like his authority or experience being questioned (which is why it's a good idea to speak with him by yourself instead of in the company of other players).

If nothing changes, you will have to decide if being a part of the team is worth your disappointment. Weigh the facts carefully, keeping in mind the following things:

♦ Drills, while they may be a bore, do work. They will strengthen your game.

◆ Even though a sport is a game, to play it well does require some discipline.

◆ If you stick with this coach now, and learn what it is he wants to teach you, you will be that much more of a skilled player. He may loosen up when he sees you've improved.

If none of this means much to you, there is the other choice: You may opt to leave the team. It may simply become clear to you that the negatives of staying on the team far outweigh the positives. You joined the team to have fun. If you're not having fun, if it isn't feeling good, if you can't see any point to the rough parts, it makes sense that you want to leave the team. You'll be giving yourself the time to play a sport you enjoy in a relaxed, less competitive atmosphere, where playing a skillful game is important but having a good time is paramount.

There may come a time when you're ready to rejoin a varsity team. Maybe you'll do it to strengthen your skills or simply because suddenly the pressure seems more exciting than burdensome. Working hard may feel more inspiring than annoying.

Whatever your reason, the important thing is that you'll be ready for the experience of varsity ball. It isn't all fun and games, but that will actually be okay by you.

A bench warmer

Q You were very excited when you made the baseball team, but something upsetting has begun to happen. The coach doesn't seem to want to use you during a game. You and the bench have become very good friends.

A Different coaches can have different attitudes about the game itself. While some view a game as an opportunity for team members to get out there, have fun, and do their best, many play only to win. Nothing else matters. They regularly use their strongest players, allowing others to spend a lot of time warming the bench.

This is an experience with which many players have had to cope. It isn't fun. It can feel anything from annoying and frustrating to insulting and humiliating. And the truth is, there's not a lot you can do about it. Certainly you can talk to your coach, but it would be best to do so with a plan in mind, not just a complaint. "I was wondering if there's a particular skill you think I could work on harder so that you would play me more" is a more effective approach than "How come you don't play me? I hate sitting on the bench all the time!" Your coach is well aware that no one likes to sit on the bench. And, your unhappiness won't get you off of it. But talking with him in a way that

HELP!

My best friend made the football team, but I didn't. I'm real embarrassed. I'm not sure I can look at him right now.

So don't. But before you back off for a while, you need to congratulate your friend. There's no point mucking up your relationship over this issue. Just tell him you're happy for him, but that you need some time alone. He'll understand. You're very disappointed and probably feeling terribly jealous and second best. It's natural. You need to allow yourself to experience those feelings.

Then, once you've wallowed a bit in your misery, remind yourself of three things:

1. You might have been off during tryouts. You can go after a place next year.

2. If your friend is the better player, it's not the worst thing in the world. There will always be people who are better at something than you. And you will always be

makes it clear you are willing to work to get off that bench might help get you the chance you want . . . especially if you work hard to get it.

Also, to make yourself feel better, you might want to consider the bigger picture.

better at something than many people around you. That's just the way it works.

3. While a lot of people may congratulate your friend, think of how many of them never even bothered to try out, knowing they didn't have a chance! You probably did have a shot. It might not have been your day, or other kids might have played particularly well. So why bother being embarrassed? You were brave and you had enough confidence to shoot for a spot.

Are you one of the younger members on the team? Perhaps next year, having been through all the practices of this one, you will be played more. Also, how does it feel to put on that uniform and wait for the very occasional opportunity to play in a real game? Are the moments a thrill? They might be worth a lot of bench warming. It's really not an insult to sit a game out. After all, you did make the team. Everyone in the stands can see that. Chances are, you're a pretty good player!

Of course, after considering all this, you might still feel that being on the team is not worth spending this much time on the sidelines. You'd rather be playing a game with your buddies than spending hours upon hours on drills and practice moves only to be told, when the real game begins, to sit it out.

That's your option and your right. And contrary to what you may fear, it doesn't make you a quitter. As suggested in the situation before this, if you joined the team to have some fun and it doesn't feel that way, it's reasonable to want to leave. This is especially true if you have been willing to put up with the drudge work in order to get to the good part, only to find that the good part never comes!

Bench warming is not so bad, if it doesn't *feel* so bad. For some people, playing the game, under whatever circumstances, is crucial. Being asked to sit out a game feels too frustrating or hurtful to bear.

If that's the case, it might be wise to quit the team. You can always try out again when either your skills improve (which means you'll have to do some serious practicing on your own) or your attitude or desires change.

Team pressure

Q You're on the school softball team and the "Casey at the Bat" syndrome is always on your mind: It's the bottom of the ninth and you're up at bat. Your team is behind by one run and the bases are loaded. But, there are two outs and you've already got two strikes against you. The crowd is going wild . . . and so is your stomach. You're desperately wishing you could fall through a hole in the ground.

Pressure is the name of this game. Everyone's eyes are on you and the pitcher. It's as if nothing else in the whole world matters except what the two of you do. And it feels as if whatever happens, the entire school will never forget it, or you.

Which simply isn't true.

You are in a tough spot. It's the kind of spot athletes find themselves in from time to time. It's actually commonplace. Obviously, when you keep score, someone has to win and someone has to lose.

Everyone watching the game knows this. They even enjoy it, because this simple arrangement adds to the thrill. The players don't always enjoy this "final" moment, however, because they are responsible for the outcome. And so the decisive run takes on HUGE significance. It can feel like the most important thing in the world, and as if the players will have to live with the outcome forever.

But they won't, and neither will you. Especially if you put this kind of high-pressure moment in perspective.

First of all, you need to remind yourself that, in truth, this is just a game. One of many. And even if it's the most important game of the season, it's still something upon which nobody's life or future depends.

Second, you need to remember that while you may be largely responsible for what happens in this final point, you are not responsible for the entire game. Other people have been involved racking up or not racking up runs, and that is a large part of why the game has come down to this crucial moment. It appears that the entire game depends on you, but that's an illusion. The entire game rests on everyone's shoulders.

Third, at a time like this, you should keep in mind your overall performance. (This point will be especially true if your sport is, for instance, tennis and it's the final point of a singles match.) There have probably been many times during this game and others in which you have come through and played terrific ball. This high-pressured moment may turn out to be one of them and it may not. But it won't decide whether or not you deserve to be on the team.

Fourth, keep in mind that most people watching are very glad they aren't you. In other words, while you might have their complete attention, and even their critical eye, you also have a degree of their sympathy. Sure, if you strike out you might hear a lot of groans, but it won't be because they think you're a loser. It will be because the game has been lost. There's a big difference.

As for how to deal with your and everyone else's feelings if you strike out, that depends on how you are most comfortable dealing with disappointment.

When the game is over, go ahead and feel bad that your team lost. You can even feel bad that you couldn't pull that last great move out of a hat. You might want to walk away and grab a few moments alone to try and collect yourself. You wanted to be the hero and somehow it didn't work out that way. That can feel pretty terrible. So let it. But don't allow yourself or anyone else to make you feel that you blew it for everyone. That's not disappointment. That's guilt, and you simply do not deserve to feel that way.

If someone gives you a tough time, be firm. "You think you could have done better?" will do nicely, and so will "Look, I feel bad enough without you blaming me for the whole game. I mean, I'm not the only player on the team!" If you don't accept the blame for the loss, no one will be able to lay it at your feet.

So, the next time you're up at bat, or ready to serve, or approaching the basket for that final free throw, remember these two basics. One, you want to try to win. Two, if you lose, it's because somebody has to. That's the rule, and there's nothing you can do to change it.

Great expectations

Q You love to play basketball, and you're good, too. The problem is you feel like you're putting on a show and that everyone expects you to make that amazing move they'll be able to talk about for weeks. You want to have fun, but game time is beginning to feel like a nightmare.

A It's very important to take a step back at this point to examine just exactly why spectators love a good game.

It's a chance to forget about problems. It's a chance to get some thrills. It's an opportunity to feel like a winner and to revel in an atmosphere of success. It's about the fan-tasy of riding into the sunset with a gold medal and the adoration of the crowds.

In short, it's about every-thing but you.

You're just a cog in ma-chinery that will hopefully work exactly right, so that the person who is watching can have a grand old time.

In a way that's a drag for

both of you. The spectator is dependent on what other people do to make himself feel good, and you have a huge crowd of people waiting for you to make them happy. Talk about impossible situations!

But that's the way it is, and the only thing you can do about it is decide to lighten up and play the game for the team, reminding yourself that everyone is dependent on each other.

Of course, that's never as easy as it sounds. For one thing, is your coach a win-win-win type, or is she most invested in the players simply doing their best? If your coach is putting too much pressure upon you, it would be a good idea to discuss this with an assistant coach, or a parent or teacher who you think might understand. They will likely try and find a way to subtly intervene and perhaps influence the coach to lighten up. If your coach remains a big part of why you feel this pressure, you might want to consider

whether staying on the team is really worth the pain.

However, if the pressure is not coming from your coach, then go speak to her! Tell her how you're feeling before each game. If she's not the type who has to win them all, chances are that as a result of the talk she will begin to communicate more clearly during practice that winning is not everything—that playing a good game is the goal no matter what the outcome—and that no single person is responsible for winning or losing a game. This will relax not only your teammates' expectations of you, but also your expectations of yourself.

Also, independent of your coach, you ought to have a talk with yourself before each game. Give yourself permission to be a good, solid player. Remind yourself that nothing spectacular is necessary. You can play your best, not be a killer out there, and still be valuable. And ask yourself, looking around at your teammates, who elected you to be their savior? No one, that's who. Your talent coupled with your teammates' insecurity about their own performances may have increased their expectations of you.

It's nice to be a hero. People like having them, and the few who achieve that status have a magical moment or two up on that pedestal. But, the only way off that pedestal is down, and sooner or later the hero has to take the plunge.

If you've played a few great games, consider yourself skilled and lucky. But keep it in perspective. Games are just a part of life. And as with all parts of life, there are ups and downs. To expect otherwise is to set yourself up for pain and disappointment that you don't deserve.

Slipping grades

Q You're on the swim team. It's taking up most of your after-school hours, which would be fine with you except for one thing: Your grades are slipping. Badly. Your teachers and parents are growing increasingly upset with you, and you don't know what to do.

A It's easy to get caught up with other people's ideas of how we should be performing. We forget to consider exactly what it is we would like for ourselves. Until you know what you want for yourself, it will be hard to find the motivation to achieve it!

Let's assume you would

like both your athletic and your school lives to be going along well. Why shouldn't you? These are your two important "jobs" and you'd probably like to feel proud of yourself in both arenas. The question is, can you?

Swimming has apparently been more important to you. If that remains so, does that have to mean your grades will slip? To begin sorting this out, consider whether or not you are handling your time to the best of your ability. When you aren't practicing with the team, are you applying yourself to your work? Is there time you are spending socializing that you might better spend in the library?

Talk to your teachers. Do they think some tutoring might help? If so, try and schedule it during whatever free time you've got. If that's impossible, ask your coach if you can come late to one or two practices until you've had a chance to catch up.

In other words, do whatever you can to achieve a bal-

ance that will still respect the team effort but also help your work.

Of course, you may not be able to have a flexible practice schedule. Your coach, for reasons of team morale as well as his or her own views on practice, may feel you have to attend each entire practice or not come at all.

In this event, you will have a decision to make. You will have to sit down and seriously consider your priorities. Obviously, if you are about to flunk out, there is no decision. School is not something you can simply "throw over" in order to pursue a sport. Or rather, you could, if you are old enough to drop out, but then you wouldn't be on the school team anymore, anyway!

The real dilemma comes when your grades are passable but are not up to your abilities. What then? What matters most?

If your parents are not pressuring you to drop the team and the decision is completely up to you, the best thing you can do for yourself is get an "education in consequences." This means that you need to learn the risks of letting your school record slip so that you can decide if they are acceptable to you.

You can get this education from reading articles about the job market, talking to any former professional athletes you might know, checking into college admission procedures, confiding in a school guidance counselor, and more. Here are a few facts you are bound to uncover:

◆ Poor grades can begin to wear away at your self-esteem. It's easy to say that swimming is the most important thing in your life, but are you willing to let it be the only *positive* thing in your life?

◆ Slacking off in your work can actually limit your world. Your sense of history or literature or geometry does affect the way you sort out

problems, and even your topics of conversation. It's nice to be known as a jock. That can have a rather terrific ring to it. But only if it's a word that's used to describe a part of you, not the whole you. Otherwise, being called a jock can imply that there's nothing else about the way you are that's worth knowing.

◆ A record of poor grades will limit your college options. While college may seem a long way off, the admissions people like to look at your academic history to get an idea of your work patterns.

If you're quite young, in eighth grade or below, you might feel a desperate need to throw yourself into the sport and worry about your grades later. This is a decision you will need to come to with some input from your parents and school counselors. In this instance, you may need to make a pact with yourself that you will not let your grades go below a certain point, and that next year you will hunker down and work hard.

However, if you are an older student, you may simply have to accept that you cannot have it all—especially if you are not intending to make sports your entire life. If you're confident of your athletic talents and don't want them to slip, then you might opt to leave the team and establish your own swim schedule while you work to get your grades up. You can always try joining the team again next year.

But here's the thing. Even if it feels like sports are going to be your whole life—that school is not a priority, and that now is the time for you to throw yourself into your athletic future—talk your decision through with someone at school, or your parents, or even someone in the professional athletic field. You will benefit from another perspective. It is very difficult to become a pro athlete. Just be-

cause it's your dream doesn't make it a strong possibility. You will want to try and honestly assess as best you can exactly how gifted an athlete you really are. What makes a star at your school doesn't necessarily make one on a national stage. Also, you may need to be made aware of how critical an education can be to a major-league athlete:

◆ A well-educated athlete usually makes smarter decisions for himself about his own training in terms of with whom, where, and under what conditions. He's learned how to research, investigate, assess, and negotiate.

◆ A well-educated athlete is not as dependent on others to make the best business decisions for her. She can calculate her own figures, read the fine print in contracts, and recognize when someone might be taking advantage of her.

♦ A well-educated athlete will one day no longer be out on the competitive field, and he will have many more options than a dropout when it comes time to fashion a different sort of work life for himself. Most ex-athletic superstars are not content merely advertising sports equipment on TV. They want to build their own successful businesses and can only do that if they have the background to do so.

Whatever you decide, however, stay open-minded. Nothing is etched in stone. You can reverse your thinking. If you drop the sport and work hard at school, you can always go back to the team at the appropriate time and try again. And if you decide the sport is most important, never think you can't change your mind. You can leave the team later and try to get those grades up as quickly as possible.

Ideally, you will think this dilemma through, correctly assess what you need, and go for it. But people change. Needs change and dreams change.

The idea is to keep thinking. Keep on top of things.

And try to always do what's best for *you*. Sure, your coach might be disappointed. Your parents might be worried or upset. But it's you who has to live with the decisions you make. And it's you who has to work toward your goals.

So choose them wisely.

You're nonathletic

Q You are the least athletic member of your crowd. You like sports but it's humiliating to play with your friends. You can tell no one really wants you on their team and sometimes they even tease you about it. You're getting to the point where you figure you better just stop trying.

A Traditionally, sports have been a way for boys to display their masculinity. Sports require speed, strength, aggressiveness, and a kind of "killer instinct." They have also always been viewed as a good way to snag a girl.

Buying into these ideas is reason enough for you to feel drawn to sports. Add to that the fact that you enjoy getting

out there with a bat, or drib-
bling a ball, and it's easy to see
why you are feeling torn.

But while it's true that

being good at sports usually
brings respect, not being the
team's Most Valuable Player
doesn't mean you should be

HELP!

**I know a lot of girls make fun of me,
saying I'm not feminine because of
the aggressive way I play ball. I don't
feel masculine. I just want to win.**

Girls usually want to be
feminine. Boys usually
want to be masculine. But
it's not always easy to define what form these qualities should take. So it's
common, especially for
kids, to fall back on stereo-
types: Girls are caring and
gentle, boys are competi-
tive and tough.

How ridiculous.

First of all, it defies
human nature. Girls want
to be the best, just as much
as boys do! And boys are
perfectly capable of being
caring and gentle. But as
noted earlier, everyone
feels safer and more secure

when everyone else dresses
or acts the same way they
do. Then they can feel
"right." Those girls who
are teasing you are probably doing so because they
are not quite comfortable
with the way they have
defined "femininity" and
so seeing you behave an-
other way makes them
question themselves.

The bottom line is that
you need to define femi-
ninity for yourself. If you
try to follow someone's
definition of the word, it
probably won't come out
feminine at all. It will just
look phony.

treated like garbage or feel worthless. Being the last chosen during gym class for a team will likely feel a little embarrassing. But it needn't wipe you off the face of the map. It's a matter of putting things in perspective. Consider these points:

♦ If you choose to continue playing softball or basketball or soccer, even though you're not the best player, give yourself an A for strength. When you go out on the field and someone teases you, laugh and call back, "Hey, give me a break! I'm trying!" If you want admiration, that's one way to get it. There is no rule that says that if a person plays a sport he or she has to be great at it. You have a right to be out on the playing field. If you claim that right with good humor and fortitude, no one should be able to take it away from you.

♦ Take a really good look at all the so-called good

players out there. Sure, probably a few are enjoying relative stardom, but the rest? A few are poor students. Others have lots of trouble getting dates. And a few more may not be well liked for any number of reasons. Good athletes certainly enjoy their success, but despite their images, they may not do so well on "the field of life." In fact, many of them, once they step off the playing field, are probably teased about their own weaknesses!

♦ Sports are not the only way to feel strong. Those are qualities that come from inside, not from kicking or hitting or throwing a ball. It's the air of confidence you carry with you that will be most appealing. The truth is, a good baseball player who doesn't like himself very much will not attract people. Perhaps you're good onstage. Maybe you enjoy painting, or are a very strong science student. If you think this is an important thing about you, so will others. If you admire your strengths, others will, too.

So, how do you most comfortably pursue a sport if your friends can't include you gracefully and you can't get comfortable with them? Well, consider this:

H E L P !

My older brother was a terrific tennis player. I'm on the team, but I'm not as good and occasionally hear people saying so. I hate the way it makes me feel.

It's very difficult living in someone else's shadow. It can make a person feel very small.

However, you don't have to live in the shadow and you don't have to feel small. It's up to you.

You can decide that you want to play as well as you can, enjoy yourself, do well for the team, and call that enough. Yes, your brother is a better tennis player. But for you tennis is simply a thing you do well. It isn't going to make you "famous." Big deal.

Or you can ask yourself why you want to place yourself in this position at all. Is it possible that you've wanted to compete with your brother's reputation? That somehow you've been running a number on yourself to measure up? That it's not other people whose voices are upsetting you, but rather your own inner voice comparing the two of you? Maybe you'd be happier competing in a sport that's free of your brother's record.

You are clearly a good athlete. You enjoy sports. Don't ruin it for yourself by playing in a shadow.

If claiming a sport is important to you, try broadening your concept of what a sport should be. Fencing, archery, billiards, biking, and horseback riding are a few sports you might not have considered before. They require different kinds of skills and may tap into sportsmanlike abilities you never knew you had. Added benefits are that you can learn or practice the sport away from the watchful eye of your friends (these sports are generally not offered at school) and yet you can refer to it as "your sport." It will become an interesting side of you that people will want to know more about and will definitely admire. But most important, it will give you a chance to view yourself as a solid athlete.

It isn't easy being a person who doesn't seem to fit a desired mold. It requires that you look in less visible places for your unique strengths. But a good athlete will not feel good about himself, either, unless he draws on other, less visible strengths that he has. Because one day that good athlete may play poorly, or be outshined by another player, or have an accident, or simply grow too old to play well. Then what good does his "mold" do for him? Not much. What will count most then is the sort of person he is, the kind of warmth and support he is able to give and get, and the other interesting and useful skills he might have. Those things don't figure into molds.

Which is why striving to fit a mold, no matter how exciting the shape and size, simply isn't worth the struggle.

Extra-
curricular
crises

Chapter **8**

Free at last! Extracurricular activities are your choice. You decide, based on your interests, which if any you would like to join. Maybe you'd like to arrange social events with other schools. Join the Social Committee! Perhaps you're fascinated by debates. Join the Debate Team! You can participate in none, one, or several. It all depends on how you choose to use your time. You won't receive grades for these activities. There will be no tests. The amount of work you have will depend upon the amount of work you commit to doing. But this is work you should enjoy doing, so it's important that you know what you're getting into.

Extracurricular activities are meant to add a dimension

to the required school curriculum. These activities, while totally elective, are formally organized. This means that a group of kids, usually with the guidance of a faculty member, form a committee or club in which they have particular goals. To accomplish these goals, usually everyone has a role. Whether your role is to study Spanish with others, play in a string quartet, run the school newspaper, or be a part of the student government, you are not functioning alone. People are counting on you. People have certain expectations of you.

And you really ought to deliver. Sometimes this will be a cinch. Sometimes it won't. (So what else is new?)

Whenever you choose a particular activity, you're saying, "This is what I want to do. This is what I like." In some ways this can feel great, in others a little overwhelming. Friends don't always understand. Balancing schoolwork, friendships, family responsibilities, and extracurricular activities can be a trial. Conflicts can arise.

What if your best friend wishes you'd spend more time with her? What if you've committed to a certain job on a committee and suddenly don't have the time? What if friends tease you about your unusual interests?

These are tricky problems, but they're worth working out. If you elected to join a group it is because you just plain wanted to. You need to honor that. Doing so will bring you lots of pleasure, which will in turn give you a really good feeling about yourself.

Only a few good things in life come without at least a little effort. Extracurricular activities should be fun, give or take a snag or two or three. Here's how to make sure you make the best extracurricular choices and have the good time you deserve.

Nonmacho interests

Q You are a basketball nut. You could play it or watch it almost all day. You like flirting with girls, dressing cool, and hanging out with your buddies. But you are also a guy who likes poetry. In fact, a poetry club has just been formed and you have decided to join it. The only thing is, you're starting to regret the decision. Your friends who don't feel the same way about poetry as you do are giving you a hard time. "So," they tease you regularly, "are you gay or something?"

A It may be difficult to believe, but your friends' taunting has relatively nothing to do with you and poetry. It has much more to do with them and their difficulty in defining exactly who *they* are.

Chances are, especially if you are a very young teen, you are very concerned about the tremendous changes happening inside of you. It's as if you can see "manhood" around the bend, but not being there yet, you wonder how and or if you will ever get there. Most kids at this age—both boys and girls—are obsessed with the idea of finally getting older, their feelings of sexuality, and the profound fear that they might never be as manly or womanly as they dream of one day being.

In fact, they aren't really even sure what being a man or woman actually means. So they start by defining it in very simple terms. It makes the whole thing much more manageable. It makes it possible for them to feel manly or womanly more quickly. Especially if everyone follows the same rules.

They think a man is someone who plays sports, acts tough, pals around with the guys, and chases girls. A man, in short, does "macho" things.

End of story.

Only that isn't the end.

People are many things inside. And all of those things need expression.

A boy who loves the rough and tumble of a good football game can easily still enjoy the lyric qualities of a beautiful poem. A boy who enjoys hanging out at the mall and flirting with girls can still cherish moments alone with his violin or in front of his easel.

There was a time when art and music and poetry were considered "feminine" pursuits. The trouble is, old ideas die hard. Though we all certainly accept now that such interests do not simply belong to one gender or another, it can still feel easier to simply embrace old notions. Boys do rough, tough things, and girls don't.

So it logically follows that anyone who defies these ideas, such as yourself, is threatening. Your friends, seeing you bravely explore other interests, are as busy watching each other as they are you. "Is he going to be teased?" they think. "Is what he's doing acceptable?" "Actually, I've always wanted to take watercolor classes. Does that still mean I'm okay? And can I let anyone know?" "Will girls still like me if I take dance lessons?" Rather than bravely trying to answer these questions for themselves out in the open, many kids resort to teasing those who dare to be different. That way they can cling

HELP!

I play with the school orchestra, but the truth is, I'm better than most of the other kids. I don't mind, only they think I'm showing off, but I'm not.

You shouldn't be ashamed of your abilities. Nor should you hide them. And you certainly shouldn't apologize for them.

The only thing you should do is use them, when in the company of the orchestra, in a matter-of-fact, controlled manner. Play when you are told, and not during those brief silences between pieces in the name of "practicing." Play what you are supposed to play, and not any flashy embellishments, which might sound good but which will be read as "showing off." And play in sync with everyone else, not with a power or dynamic that overpowers the other instruments.

If the orchestra leader asks that you play a particular riff on your own, or suggests that you give your part more color while another

to the group. They do all the acceptable things, and most of all keep themselves out of the limelight while they try to figure out just exactly what being a "man" means.

Of course, in the process they are neither fulfilled nor filled with confidence. What

instrument recedes, that's one thing. Follow his instructions. The kids will know where it's coming from. But make no musical decisions of that nature on your own.

And next time you are bugged by a fellow musician, simply say something like, "Music's my thing. What can I do? I love it," and then turn away. You'll have reminded him of something really crucial. You're not playing well so everyone can feel bad. You're playing well because you just enjoy it.

That's hard to resent.

they are is scared—of their own interests that don't fit the macho picture, of each other's rejection, and of your ability to take a stand.

The truth is, behind all of their teasing, these friends of yours are probably admiring your courage.

It isn't easy to say, "I don't need to follow a crowd. There are some things I like to do no matter what anyone thinks." And it is especially not easy to choose something to which so many kids attach such silly meaning, right when you're trying to figure out who you are yourself.

So keep up the bravery. Recognize that your sexuality is being called into question only because your friends are concerned about their own. You needn't tell them this. But you might say, "Look, I just like poetry. It's no big deal. I'll see you on the baseball field Saturday at ten o'clock," and then walk away. Don't argue. Don't defensively reply, "I'm not gay. Stop it!" That will give their accusation too much

attention. Too much respect. Besides, your sexual orientation is none of their business. Gay or not, there is nothing about you that is wrong. Defend your interest, not your sexual feelings.

And by the way, in the process of growing into your sexual self, you yourself might indeed wonder if you have gay tendencies. You may be aware of feelings that you have deep inside you about both boys and girls. Rest assured that these feelings are perfectly normal. Everyone has them. It's just that not everyone is willing to recognize the confusion inside themselves.

You may turn out to be gay, and you may not. Whether you do or not has absolutely nothing to do with whether or not you enjoy poetry or whether or not you are aware of confused feelings about boys and girls. So don't be afraid to feel what you naturally feel and don't be afraid to pursue the interests that you have.

You owe it to yourself to find out exactly who you are, and that can only happen if you give yourself the freedom to do so.

Keeping your own i.d.

Q You hang around with a very cool crowd. It makes you feel special. But you have some interests they do not share. You are dying to join the Debate Team, but you just know your friends will think it's really weird. In fact, you're pretty sure they will start to lose interest in you.

A Again, it's much safer to define oneself by following a group. If everyone does the same thing, likes the same thing, and appears to think the same way, everyone is safe. Somehow it feels as if that means everyone is right. Everyone is strong. And most important, everyone will keep liking each other.

But of course it means no such thing. It really only means that everyone is insecure and anxious to please each other!

Extracurricular activities are an opportunity for you to explore something that means a lot to you. Something your academic schedule doesn't include. Something your teachers don't have the time to teach or explore with you. They provide a chance to band together with kids who have the same specific interests. This can be tremendously exciting. It is your right to join in and make the most of the skills, talents, and interests that you have. They are part of what make you special and interesting.

Naturally, then, the question is, if you can't let your crowd know about your interests, exactly how good are these friends? If they only want you if you can make yourself look, feel, and act as they do, how terrific is that?

Certainly you've thought of this yourself. But somehow belonging to a crowd just seems at times more important than pursuing an interest, no matter how powerful. Being a member of that crowd seems more urgent than the expression of who you really are.

It's not hard to understand why. So many things are happening to you physically, emotionally, and intellectually as you mature that it's easy to cling to a crowd as if it were a lifeboat.

The problem is, sometimes groups are not the lifeboat they seem to be. Ironically, they can instead be a place where members are required to drown all the parts of themselves that make them special.

So you have a few decisions to make. One, do you want to be a member of a crowd that would reject you for not being just like them? (Not all crowds are like that, by the way!) Two, is being a member of this crowd more important than your interest in the Debate Team? And three, do you have the courage to stand up for who you are and see what happens? It's not a crime if you don't. This may not be the time to battle it out with the crowd or look for new friends.

The most important thing to keep in mind in this situation is the truth about *you*. Who are you? What do you like? What do you dream about? This may not be the time to take a stand. But sooner or later you will have to address the many parts of you that need expression and that make you special. Otherwise you will never be happy.

Extracurricular activities at school are a chance to express your individual interests. They aren't mandatory, and so they require you to stand up and say, "Yes. I'm interested very much in that." People will notice. Part of how they react is completely out of your control. Still, one thing you can say if your interests are questioned is simply, "Hey. I'm still the same person! I just happen to like debating!"

Because really, it's kind of ridiculous. Why should it matter to your friends what you like, as long as it can't get you or them in trouble, it doesn't hurt anyone, and most of all, you still like them?

Job jealousy

Q You are a talented writer and have dreams of one day being a journalist. You would like to have a column reporting on different issues for the school paper. The problem is, an upperclassman already has that position. You think you can actually write better than she can, and are very annoyed that you are stuck with the uninspiring "Week in Review" paragraph.

A It's good to think you deserve things. That way you are motivated to get them. But life is neither easy nor fair. You can't always get what you deserve, and if you do get it, it may not come exactly when you want it. Also, you may think you deserve something, but think-

---

I should have won for V-P of my school, but the girl who won is really pretty and super-friendly and flirts with all the guys. I'm furious! I've served on lots of committees and know much more about student government.

Anyone involved in politics will tell you that the best-qualified candidate does not necessarily win. That's because voters are often swayed by things other than, for instance, who has a record of raising taxes, or caring for the environment, or backing off from campaign promises. Instead, voters go with other impressions. Who seems more likable? More real? Who seems to care the most and have a charming personality to boot?

Still, despite these facts —which *are* out of your control—it will be helpful to consider how you might have put your own best foot forward in a stronger way. There may be other campaigns in your future!

Political candidates these days know that, with all the TV coverage, they've got to put forth more than their stands on different issues. They have to work on putting themselves across. For you, at your school, where everyone can see you every day, this is a constant issue. It's possible

ing so doesn't make you right.

Why? Because other people share this world with you.

that you forgot to project the kind of image that would have equalled, in its own way, that of your rival. Then again, maybe working on your image is simply not something that interests you. You think issues are key, not how you look or sound.

Give this some thought. You may discover that losing was just as well. You can now work in a satisfying and less image-dependent way on the issues that are most important to you. But if you don't mind working on projecting a friendlier you, then keep in mind that there will always be other elections.

And the time to start working is now!

They deserve and want things, too. Sometimes they even want the same things you do. At the same time. Just as badly.

So it logically follows that not everyone is going to walk away happy. Someone is going to win, and someone will lose. Or, as in the situation above, someone is going to have to wait his or her turn.

In this case it's you.

Which brings us to another fact of life. Talent is not the only thing people need to get ahead. They need to get along well with others. They need to recognize their own weaknesses. They need patience and tenacity.

This older student probably has some ability as well or she wouldn't hold the position that she does. She's probably worked hard to get where she is. You need to respect what she's learned and where she's been. You need to let her see that. It will inspire her to teach you a few things you may not know. You need to accept the position that you are given, no matter how small, and keep working at it so that you can prove—and improve—your talent so that next year you will be given more responsibility. Remember, patience and tenacity are key.

It's one thing to have confidence in yourself. It's another to shove it down people's throats, and/or to try and shove other people aside. We all have things to learn from others who are more experienced. Even if you are more talented than the current reporter, you may not know as much about tailoring an article to fit a certain space, or even about specific reporting techniques.

Yes, you probably joined the newspaper so you could realize your dream, and now you're frustrated and disappointed. But chances are, everyone who joined the paper, even those a year or two before you, did so to realize

their dreams, too. Probably the reporter you now envy used to have your column and was just as frustrated by the person who had her current spot!

But she waited it out, and here she is.

Well, you have to pay your dues, too. It's only fair. She put in her time; she deserves the glory. Sure, you may prove to be a better reporter when your time comes. But that doesn't mean you should have been the reporter all along. For one thing, you have lots to learn, and for another, extracurricular activities exist for everyone to have a chance.

It's good to set goals and to strive to reach them. But just because you elect to do something doesn't mean the whole world will sit up and take notice. Sometimes you have to work very hard for what you want . . . no matter how deserving you may be.

Losing the lead

Q You and a friend tried out for the school play. Both of you were anxious to win the lead, though neither of you voiced it to the other. Now the casting list has been posted, and your friend has won the lead. You have a nice part, but it's neither as big nor as romantic as your friend's, and you feel disappointed and embarrassed.

A The theater can be a very exciting and glamorous place. But anyone who has elected to become a part of the "scene" will also tell you it has a lot of painful, difficult moments.

When it comes to putting on a show, you are doing so in accordance with someone else's vision. The author of the play or musical has invested the various characters with certain physical and emotional qualities. The director of the play brings his or her own interpretations of these characters to his direction. The person in charge of casting brings his or her ideas together with the director's to the task of selecting what appears to be the right person for the specific part.

Which all comes down to one simple thing. Your individual strengths or gifts will often not be a match

HELP!

My good friend got a big part in the school play, but I didn't get one at all. I feel sick.

You feel sick because it feels like you've just been told your friend can act but you can't.

In truth, all you've been told is that there is no part for you in this particular play. Naturally, if every time you auditioned for a play you repeatedly got no parts, you might want to consider the possibility that acting is not your strength. But one "no thanks" means nothing. It just feels awful, especially because you can't commiserate with your friend. She's thrilled and you're not.

Congratulate her, and then go find another friend's shoulder to cry on. Next, think about getting involved in lighting or set construction. If you're around enough, you'll get a chance to listen to the director criticize and applaud his actors and actresses. You'll learn things that could enhance your acting skills.

for the specific character a playwright, director, casting director, or even musical director might have in mind. It doesn't mean you can't sing or dance or act well enough. It does mean the overall you that you bring to the stage does not seem to

Chances are, the next play will contain a role that is just right for you. But if it appears that there is no character for which you are the obvious match, think about dressing for a particular part during the audition and rehearsing a walk, smile, or laugh that would seem right for the role. You can't leave everything to a director's imagination. She may need a little help in seeing that you would make a perfect angry old woman, despite your ordinarily angelic smile!

mesh well with the character in question.

Actor Fred Savage could not have played Macaulay Culkin's part in *Home Alone* because he doesn't look or act as vulnerable as Macaulay. But they're both good actors! Roseanne would not have made a good Catwoman in *Batman Returns* because she is not as feline as Michelle Pfeiffer. But both actresses are really talented!

As for your smaller role, the fact is, audiences notice anyone onstage who is good. Lead parts do not guarantee that the people who have them will receive all the attention. People who bring something special to their roles are always noticed—sometimes even more than the so-called star. It's critical that you give your all to your part, not just because it is your responsibility to both yourself and the other players, but because it is a chance to display your talent. It will be remembered. The next time a lead part comes up that seems to fit your "type," you will stand a better chance of landing the role.

As for feeling embarrassed, or "less than," or like "a loser" next to your friend, keep in mind that she did not win a victory. No one won and no one lost. This is not about who did the best audition, or who is the better actress. This is about who fits the part best. While it's true that a good actress can transform herself to fit many different kinds of roles, even she is limited by certain qualities that to some extent "type" her. (Bette Davis, at the time of the famous casting for *Gone With the Wind,* did a screen test. She wanted the part very badly, and perhaps she might have done a good job. But the powers that be just didn't think she seemed right. And after many talented famous actresses tried out, they finally selected a virtually unknown actress for the part. And in truth, Vivien Leigh was unforgettable.)

If you want to be onstage, you have to realize that every audition carries with it the chance for rejection. Many people drop out of theater life because it's simply too hard to take. Others believe in themselves so strongly that they weather the rejections, with ever-growing determination.

A young, inexperienced Clark Gable was rejected by a major studio with the simple words, "Can't act." He didn't let that stop him. At least *you* got a part!

You're too bossy

Q You have been elected chairman of the Social Committee. You have a vice-chairman and eight other members on your committee. Your goals are to organize a fall dance, a charity fund-raiser, and a winter holiday party, and you're moving a mile a minute. Suddenly you receive a phone call from your very unhappy vice-chairman. "You're very bossy," she snaps at you. "You're trying to control everything." You couldn't be more surprised.

A A little power is a very exciting thing. This is especially true if you have the sort of personality that likes to control things. In fact, the expression "drunk on power" is very apt here, because sometimes people lose track of what's going on around them. They're so busy doing, planning, and making decisions that they forget to consult. They forget to consider the opinions of others. They forget to show some respect for the abilities of people on their team.

In short, they act like obnoxious lone rangers.

As a result, they offend the people with whom they are supposed to be working and often don't do as good a job as they might have if they had welcomed the skills and energy of those who could have helped. Ironically, their desire to control everything so it can be done just right often results in a lackluster job.

An important part of being the head of an extracurricular group is learning to work with a team and to delegate power. Some of the most effective leaders in the world are those who allow others to do their jobs while keeping themselves available for advice, debate, and support. Not only does this allow more work to get done, it also gives those people under you the respect they deserve. This in turn makes them feel happy and proud and very motivated to keep working hard. Delegating power is a way of saying, "I know you can do the job." That's a compliment.

If you're having trouble doing this, you need to take a moment to figure out why you can't let go. Is it because you're afraid that if you don't do the job it won't get done right? If so, consider what's just been said. But perhaps it's because you're afraid to face the skills of others. Perhaps you feel if they prove to be capable it will somehow diminish your own skills. If this is the case, try to remember that no two people's talents are precisely the same, and the more motivated and capable the people are, the better the job will turn out. Also, perhaps you somehow equate giving out responsibilities to losing your authority. But nothing could be further from the truth! You will actually *gain* authority by being the one to whom everyone reports.

But you will certainly begin to lose authority if everyone grows to resent the power you refuse to share!

If it appears to you that your vice-chairman was speaking on behalf of everyone on the committee, it would be wise to call a meeting and apologize. There's no need to grovel. "It's been brought to my attention that I've been acting as if I'm the only person on this team. I don't feel that way, and I'm sorry. I just got very wound-up. How about if we discuss what each person should be responsible for?"

The bottom line? Lighten up and back off. Everyone is on this committee because they want to do something, too! So let them! You were elected the head of the committee. No one will want your job as long as you let them do theirs.

No time for friends

Q You've recently joined the Chamber Music Club. You love the flute and are enjoying your commitment to the club. You're not exactly friends with the kids with whom you play, but it doesn't seem to matter. You all get along just fine. The trouble is, you and your friends are having a falling out. They resent the amount of time you've taken from them to play your music.

A You have a right, and in fact you obviously have a need, to pursue time with your music. This is something that deserves respect. It might feel as if you need to make a choice between the Chamber Music Club and your friends, but you don't. Actually, there is no choice.

What there is, is sensitivity and caring. Use them both and you should be able to straighten out your problems ...at least with those kids who, for all the right reasons, truly are your friends.

First of all, you need to try and understand what might be going on. There are many possibilities. One, some of your friends might feel jealous and threatened by your interest or talent. They might fear there is nothing special about them. Two, a few of your friends might simply need to feel that you are always available to them. Perhaps they are very insecure and need your constant attention in order to be sure of your affection. Three, several friends may not be as interested in you as they are in the group as a whole. The fact that you've changed the dynamics of the crowd by getting busy with other things has upset the way everyone defines the group. They'd rather see you out of the group than chance others doing their own thing, leaving everyone with a con-

fused sense of who they are.

The question is, what do you do about all this?

If the problem is that your friends are threatened by your talent or interest, you might refrain from constantly discussing music with them, and openly and actively encourage them to pursue things they like. Help your friends see what's special in them. They'll begin to worry less about your assets.

If the problem is that your friends are worried you won't care as much about them, take a long, honest look at your behavior. Have you been forgetting to ask them about important issues in their lives? Have you been absentminded when they speak to you? Have you had to cancel dates? If so, stop it. Friends are invaluable. You cannot allow an outside interest to take over your life.

However, if you don't feel you've been short-changing

your friends, then perhaps what you need to do is extend yourself. Put in a little extra effort to communicate how much you still care. Invite them all over for a sleepover and, in advance, bake some great cookies. Make sure you give one or the other a call at night, even if you have nothing particular to say. "Just wanted to check in" is a nice thing for a friend to hear. It means you are thinking about her.

As for what to do if your friends are more concerned about their group as a whole than each other as separate human beings, you can do two things: You can find another group, or you can try and talk to this one. The latter is preferable, of course, because chances are there is some real affection between you and your friends. Be sure you acknowledge those feelings clearly and refrain from insisting your friends have done something wrong. "I care about you guys a lot and so I think we need to talk. I feel as if you don't think it's okay

that I joined this music group. I really love it, but I love spending time with you, too." When you are through, listen. Chances are, your friends will want to tell you how they feel.

Admit it when they are right. "It's true. I can't go out for a soda on Wednesday afternoons anymore." But nicely deny it when they are wrong. "I was really sorry not to be able to go for that bike ride with you, but I had to practice. I told you that way in advance. I wish I could have done both." Then explain how you feel about your music. Tell them how it makes you feel, and about what you might like to one day do with music. In other words, bring them into your experience. Doing all of this will help your friends see you're still a good friend but that you have a side to you they didn't know about before.

Hopefully, as a result of this conversation, your friends will give you more room to be who you are. In fact, they might even do the same for themselves! But if they can't do either, you might have to simply move on to a new set of friends.

Certainly that's easier said than done. But it's a lot simpler than trying to deny who you are.

Ready to quit

Q You've been a member of the French Club for about a month. Somehow you thought you'd enjoy it more. You thought the trips to museums would be fun and the chance to speak nothing but French exciting. Unfortunately the pleasure has worn off. You'd like to just quit, but it feels as if that would be wrong.

A People do make mistakes. Perhaps the French Club is not what you hoped it would be. Perhaps you are not quite as interested in the French language and culture as you had thought. That's okay. You are in school to learn about yourself. What's important is how you handle this "mistake."

First of all, is it really a mistake? Sure, you may not be as interested in what's going on as you thought, but is it possible that you could actually make things more interesting for yourself? Perhaps you haven't taken enough of a lead in designing some activities that would be educational and fun for you. Some extracurricular activities provide a unique opportunity for you to decide how to educate and inspire | yourself. It isn't like the classroom, where the teacher deter-

H E L P !

I'm on the Community Outreach Committee. Lately people have been dropping out because they think it's too much work. It makes me really mad.

Sometimes people join a committee thinking it will be both a responsible thing to do and fun. Then they find out it's mostly work, so they want to quit because school and other responsibilities are hard enough. There really isn't much you can do about it. At this point in your life, for your own reasons, you are motivated to help others. The students who are dropping out are not. This could be so for lots of reasons. They may have trouble with schoolwork, problems at home, too many outside activities, and any number of other issues going on in their lives. Sure, quitting in the middle is not a responsible move, but don't allow yourself to pass judgment on these students. It could lose you lots of friends!

Do the best you can with the kids that are left on your committee. Instead of putting together a big holiday party, design a smaller one.

Most of all, allow people to do what they can.

Getting mad at what they can't do won't help the community, the other kids, or you.

mines the lesson plan. So let your mind run free. You might just find you can turn this club experience into something wonderful.

If it really is a case of simply not enjoying "things French" as much as you thought you might, then you will of course want to leave the club. But before you do, consider whether or not you had any particular responsibilities that would place the other members in a difficult position if you left. If so, you should try and time your departure so that it does not negatively affect the other kids. If you were planning a French Club bake sale and you were supposed to make éclairs, then make them. If you were going to be responsible for decorations for a Friday afternoon cabaret, then do them. Once you have fulfilled your club responsibilities, then you can consider your own needs.

As for how you leave, you ought to do so sensitively and with some explanation to the other members. It isn't nice

or fair to simply disappear. Though that may seem like the easy way out, it isn't. You will likely run into those students many times during the day, and you can't just run away. The best thing to do is be tactful yet honest. "I guess I thought I wanted to spend more time on French issues than I actually do" or "I enjoyed this, but I'm very interested in tennis and music, too, and I just don't have time for everything" would do nicely. The important thing is to make sure they don't feel at fault. That wouldn't be fair. Just because you got bored doesn't mean they aren't interesting.

Finally, don't torture yourself about having left. You had every right to give it a try. That's how a person learns about what he or she likes and doesn't like. You just don't have a right to step on other people's needs while you fulfill your own. If you leave the club gracefully and in a responsible manner, no one, including yourself, should hold it against you.

Chapter 9

Physical fears

"The world is not a safe place."

Certainly you've heard people say these words before. They are usually uttered in response to a threat of some sort. Perhaps it's an environmental issue, or a criminal act, or a virulent illness, or news of a civil war in some faraway country.

Or maybe it's in response to something that has happened almost literally in your own backyard. Or at school.

It would be positively wonderful if all students could view their school as a safe, secure place. And in fact, many do. Each day they get on the bus, enjoy a safe ride to school, and, once inside, concern themselves with such matters as getting along with friends, worrying about grades, consulting with teachers, competing in sports, and all the other issues described in this book so far.

But unfortunately there are many students in this country for whom such concerns are a luxury. What they worry about is staying physically safe. There is always a feeling of violence in the air, and while it may not rear its ugly head on a daily basis, the threat of it is always present. It is an oppressive, frightening, and depressing fact of school life.

In fact, in many ways it can ruin the entire experience.

Sadly, there are no easy answers. You are too young to control another student's behavior. In most cases, you cannot stop someone from taking his anger out on other people if that is what he chooses to do. To be honest, you cannot even totally protect yourself. If you are being cornered by a crowd, or chased by someone, or hurt or abused emotionally or physically, there are no foolproof steps you can take to end the confrontation.

But despite the way that sounds, you are still not completely helpless.

Much of what you can do to keep yourself safe falls into a three-step plan. Stay ALERT, always ANTICI-PATE, and ask for HELP.

As you read through this chapter you will come to see that there are things you can do to separate yourself from potentially violent incidents. These methods are not a cure for your fears. (In fact, ridding yourself of fear might be unsafe. It's the fear that signals the need for alertness and anticipation.) These methods are, however, your "weapons" against becoming a victim. As stated before, while you cannot control someone else's ill will toward you, you can control to some extent the circumstances that might provoke an expression of violence.

Of course, violence is not the only threat to physical safety that students fear. There's also AIDS.

This sexually transmitted disease is a threat to students in every school, no matter how peaceful and harmonious the atmosphere. Unfortunately, many kids don't realize this. If the community they live in feels safe and protected, they somehow assume that AIDS and other sexually transmitted diseases can't touch or harm them.

Wrong.

The good news is that you can protect yourself from AIDS. But, you need knowledge to do so. You need to know how the disease is transmitted. You need to understand why even you are a potential victim. Your friends need to know, too. Finally, you need to know what you can and cannot do with a friend who is HIV positive or has AIDS. By virtue of this knowledge and your mutual sense of responsibility toward each other, you will protect each other—you from the vio-

lence of contamination and he or she from the violence of rejection.

True, the world is not a safe place. But that doesn't mean you're helpless. What it does mean is that you have to play it smart. You have to understand the world in which you live. You have to be aware of the rage inside a student so that you don't ignite it. And you must know the truth about contagious diseases so that they are not allowed to spread.

You can do these things. You cannot protect yourself completely from life's cruel or unjust moments. But you can minimize your vulnerability. You do have the power to feel safer in what might feel like a very unsafe school.

Here's how.

On the school bus

Q The school bus ride scares you. There is no monitor because the kids are older (fifth grade and up), and there are a number of scary students who ride the bus. The driver seems to ignore them, even when they pick fights with other students. The other day you even heard one of the boys making rude and frightening remarks to a very distressed girl.

A You have a right to be scared. The bus is not always a safe place. For one thing, it's a moving vehicle operated by one person. If he or she were to be distracted by any dangerous activity on the bus, everyone could get hurt. In an ideal situation the driver would be able to bring the bus to a safe stop and then break up whatever problem is brewing. But to be honest, that does seem to depend on the driver and how he sees his job. Some just keep driving no matter what the problem. Others feel it's up to them to step in and interrupt trouble. In other words, in most communities bus drivers are not required to behave like police officers.

Second, it's a closed space. You can't just run away. You can't jump off a moving bus, and most people on the street will not be able to see what is going on inside. Only the passengers have a clear view.

Still, in terms of staying alert, anticipating problems, and asking for help, there are definite steps you can take to protect yourself.

◆ Stay alert: Keep your eyes and ears open. If it appears to you that some rough kids are giving you the eye, look away. Don't stare. Don't call attention to yourself. Stick with a few close friends, or keep to yourself.

◆ Anticipate: It's probably safer to sit as close to the front as you can. Most trouble begins toward the back, where students feel the driver is a safe distance away.

◆ Ask for help: Once you are at school, speak to the principal. Report clearly and as accurately as you can what has been going on in the bus. You can request that your name not be used in discussions he might have with others about the situation. Hopefully the principal will assign a monitor to the bus. If he cannot or does not, you might want to discuss the matter with your parents. (You should tell them what is going on anyway, even if the principal can effect some quick action.) They may in turn be able to organize a group of parents who could take the matter to the school board or a government official.

There's a saying that goes, "The squeaky wheel gets the grease." If you raise your voice loud enough, you and the other terrorized kids on the bus will get some help. And you should. Violence on your school bus is a very dangerous situation. It's a bad idea to wait for something dreadful to happen before asking for help. People need to speak out before someone becomes a victim.

That someone, after all, could be any one of them. Even you.

Hassled in the hallway

Q You are afraid to walk around the hallways of your school. A number of students have already been hassled by a few difficult kids, and you don't want to be next.

The best advice to follow is, be where you are supposed to be. If you stick to your school schedule, you will likely never find yourself alone and vulnerable to an attack. Most kids who are out to hurt or bully someone will not seek to do so in a crowded place.

Sometimes, of course, you can't keep exactly to your schedule. Things come up. You need to use the bathroom. You have a conference scheduled with a teacher after school lets out. You need to bring a note somewhere. Consider the following tips for beefing up your personal safety.

♦ Whatever you do, stay alert: Watch the way you relate to others.
♦ Anticipate the problem: If you know there have been incidents in the bathroom, or suspect the possibility, try requesting that your principal place a monitor there. If you are between classes, see if a friend will come with you.
♦ Ask for help: If you must bring a note somewhere during class hours, quietly express your fears and request that another student be allowed to accompany you.
♦ Similarly, if you have an appointment with a teacher after school, ask him or her to escort you to the front door of the school when the meeting is over. Try not to go anywhere alone.

The truth is, while there are angry kids out there who would strike out at practically anybody, for the most part they will choose their victims for a "reason." The person they choose to frighten may either look easy to intimidate, or may be someone they claim to have a grudge against. It could be a very small thing that transpired between them, but it's used as sufficient excuse. If you stare too long at an angry student, making him self-conscious, he might think that's ample reason to strike out. If you smile when she's unable to answer a question in class, she might decide you need to be "taught a lesson."

While we are all potential victims (regrettably, anything could happen to any of us), there are steps you can take to keep from being a target. Don't draw attention to yourself, and don't move around the school alone. If you can manage these two things, chances are you'll be fine.

HELP!

This real scary kid came over to me the other day and said, "Are you staring at me?" I wasn't. He wanted to start a fight. Luckily the bell rang, but what do I do if he does it again?

Don't run. Don't turn away. Stay as calm as you can, look him in the eye, and say, "I wasn't staring at you." If he insists you were, repeat what you've said matter-of-factly. "I mean it. I wasn't staring at you." Then, as soon as the opportunity arises, walk away.

This person is picking a fight using words instead of a punch. The best way to defuse it is by using the same weapon. If you sound calm and refuse to get drawn into a verbal battle, he will likely give up. In war terms, he would have been "unable to engage the enemy!"

Running for help

Q You are late arriving to school, and just as you reach the front steps you notice a friend of yours being beaten up by a few guys. No one else is around, and it is clear your friend needs help fast.

A Movie heroes look great. They look strong, brave, and exciting. They win friends, they get the girl, and they come out on top.

Real heroes often don't fare so well. Often this is because they simply take on more than they should. Their hearts are in the right place, but they simply don't have the strength, backup, or luck to help them save the day.

You can't script life. So don't make the mistake of thinking that you can. Instead, recognize the truth.

You are only one person. And chances are, not yet a very

big or physically mature person either. If you see a friend getting beaten up by some kids, you will have to assume you alone cannot save your friend. In fact, it's the only safe thing to conclude, both for his sake and yours. Otherwise you'd be inviting more trouble than already exists.

◆ If you were to enter the fray you might get beaten up just as badly. Your friend is not likely to be much help, as he is probably upset, weakened, and perhaps even injured.

◆ If you were to enter the fray, the attackers might get especially worked up, and might become even more violent.

◆ If you were to enter the fray, you would be unable to do the one thing that someone has to do—and quickly. You

---

H E L P !

If I see someone getting beaten up by a bunch of guys, as I run for help should I scream, "HELP!"?

When in doubt, don't yell, "HELP!" You need to stay safe until you can get the help that is needed. If you scream and there are many kids involved, some may come after you. This could place you in danger, make it impossible for you to get help, and bring the violence already being visited on the other student to a frenzied level.

If, however, you feel that you've got to say something before running, you can try yelling very loudly, "Hey! The police are coming!" The attackers will likely become scared and confused, and as a result run.

would be unable to go for help.

The best thing you can do for your friend (or anyone else you see in this sort of danger) is go get help. "Help" in this instance would be people who could put

an end to the attack. Run into the school, head straight for the first office you can get to, and loudly ask that someone help. Don't be shy. Don't wait for someone to notice you. And don't forget the facts. Tell them where to go quickly and clearly.

And then, be there to help and comfort your friend. Let him talk about how he feels both physically and emotionally. Other people will tend to his wounds, but he will also need someone to listen to how upset or frightened or violated he feels. We often forget that people who are victims of physical abuse don't just need attention to their bodies. They also need attention to their minds and hearts.

If you run and get the help your friend needs quickly, and if you are there to help him recover in every way, then to him you will be a real hero.

And just like in the movies, you will, in your way, come out on top.

Reporting others

Q You are aware that a group of students are planning something bad. You think it will involve roughing up another student or even a teacher. You don't know what to do. You're pretty sure they want to hurt someone, but you're afraid if you tell on them, it might end up being you.

A If there is violence in your school, chances are it feels to you as if things are completely out of control; as if there is no one who can take over whom you can trust. But that is very unlikely. There are probably a number of adults in your school in whom you can confide this difficult information without inviting trouble for yourself. Just because there are kids in your school who are out of control, does not mean that everyone else is. It simply means that it's impossible to make everyone toe the line. There will always be some students who for reasons of their own simply refuse to do so. That doesn't mean they can't be outsmarted or outmaneuvered by people who are lucky enough to know what's up.

Select the adult in your

school you feel closest to and tell him or her what you know. It can be a teacher, a counselor, a school psychologist, or even the principal. Be clear about the facts. What exactly have you heard? What leads you to believe it will involve some form of physical violence? It's important to separate out what you know from what you suspect. It's scary attending a school that has problems with violence. It's easy to fear the worst so deeply that it feels as if it's inevitable. But it may not be, and to present it as otherwise might get innocent students in trouble. But that doesn't mean you should keep your fears to yourself.

Absolutely not.

It just means you should be clear about what you *heard* as opposed to what you *think.* The person in authority who investigates the matter will find the entire picture useful in stopping a real problem as well as in anticipating others.

And of course, be sure to tell this person you would like your name kept out of the picture. He or she would more than likely do this anyway, but it will help you feel more sure.

Finally, remember this. If you do nothing about something you hear, or something you suspect, and the worst does happen, you will probably feel pretty terrible. Not that you will be responsible for the incident, because you won't be. But school, just like a small town, is a community. And just as neighbors are supposed to keep an eye out for each other, so should the students of a school. If someone you knew suspected you might be getting into trouble, you would hope that they would find a way to safely warn you. You wouldn't necessarily expect them to place themselves in danger, but you would certainly want them to do something to help. Well, your schoolmates deserve the same assistance from you.

You owe it to them, and you owe it to yourself.

Witnessing an attack

Q You've just witnessed a student being attacked with a knife by another student. It is perhaps the most frightening thing you've ever seen, and now you are terribly depressed. It seems to you that you will never be able to walk anywhere again and feel safe . . . and that people are basically horrible creatures.

A It is true that all of us—even you—are capable of violent acts. Thankfully, however, most of us choose not to give in to these impulses. We choose not to because the anger necessary to fuel a violent act is not overwhelming, or rather, it is balanced by other, more positive feelings. (Also we have the control to remind ourselves that destructive acts bring serious punishments.) Our knowledge that family members love us and want to see us grow and learn, often inspires us to be helpful to others. And the sense that we exist in a world in which we can make our dreams happen, gives us the belief that others have the same right.

But there are many students in your school who may not have had these positive experiences. They cannot control themselves. They may not feel as if they are cared for. They may have no one encouraging them, and may in fact be treated rather brutally at home. And finally, they may be living in circumstances in which it seems that dreams are a useless, painful pastime.

It is usually these students who choose to use violence. They are seething with anger, disappointment, and frustration, and in an effort to give some expression to these feelings, they strike out. They seek to hurt others because they are hurting inside.

Of course, students who commit violent acts may not be aware of exactly why they've chosen this route. They may claim their behavior is "cool" or "tough" or any number of other things that allow them to feel strong. Hearing their boasts can be especially frightening to you. You might think, "There are such mean, uncaring people

in this world." And in a way you're right. But at their core, all those mean, uncaring people are really very hurt people.

Knowing this might help you feel less depressed about the state of mankind, and perhaps just a little more hopeful. This does not excuse violent behavior. People don't have the right to hurt others just because they have been hurt themselves, unless it's an act of self-defense. But it helps to explain violent behavior in another, less threatening light.

Finally, if the effect of what you saw between those two students does not recede, it's important to get help from a counselor. People forget that criminal acts affect more than just the people directly involved. It can hurt the onlookers, too. It can make them feel scared, depressed, angry, and also horribly frustrated at their inability to stop the trouble. Witnesses are victims, too. Your pain is a common and understandable reaction to witnessing a violent act. You need to give it the attention it deserves.

And then remember how the whole incident began. It began from hurt. Perhaps you can decide to volunteer some time to a youth organization for very young kids. And one day, when you draw a little child onto your lap and give him a hug, you can say to yourself, "Maybe this child, because of this hug, will be a little less hurt today . . . and a little less violent tomorrow." There is hope. But some people need a little extra help finding it.

Frightened of AIDS

Q You have heard rumors in your school that a student in your class has AIDS. You don't know if it's true or not, but you can't help looking at everyone very suspiciously. In fact, you really don't know why the school doesn't just tell you who it is, so that you can be sure to steer clear of that person.

A Your school is protecting the sick student's right to privacy. Contrary to what you might fear, this need not compromise your safety. AIDS is a disease that attacks the victim's immune system. It attacks his, or hers, but not yours, unless you place yourself in very particular circumstances with this person. You and your friends can enjoy everyday social interactions with the student who has AIDS, and still stay healthy. Because of this, his or her right to privacy is deemed the first concern.

The fact is, you cannot get AIDS by sitting in class next to a person who has it. You cannot get AIDS by talking to him or going to the movies with him or even going to gym with him. You cannot get AIDS from hugging her or trading clothes with her or even using the toilet directly after her.

It has been medically proven that you can't.

However, AIDS is a disease that can be transmitted to others under certain circumstances. You do not want to be in a position to exchange bodily fluids. These fluids are semen, blood, and saliva (which is a bodily fluid but not necessarily one that carries HIV, or human immunodeficiency virus—the virus associated with AIDS).

What does this mean? AIDS can be passed from one person to another through the act of sexual intercourse. Don't have unprotected sex; it's even safer to practice abstinence. If you know you are going to engage in physical intimacy, be very sure you know all the important things there are to know about your partner before you act. Has he or she had previous sexual partners? Has he or she ever taken any drugs intravenously? (Bodily fluids can be exchanged if needles were shared.)

Do keep in mind that asking these questions does not guarantee you honest answers. It's critical that you really get to know a person well before you consider any intimate act. You'll be better able to evaluate what's true and what isn't and thus protect yourself both physically and emotionally from hurt. When it comes to AIDS, there's a saying that when you sleep with a person you are also sleeping with everyone else he or she has ever slept with. Simply translated, this means your boyfriend or girlfriend might be HIV positive and not know it, because a while back he or she slept with someone who was also HIV positive and may or may not have known it. HIV attacks the immune system. If a person is

---

H E L P !

My parents won't let me hang out with a friend who just found out he has HIV, which he got from a blood transfusion. They won't listen to a word I say about the medical facts.

There is no cure for AIDS yet, and as a result people are terrified. Your parents want to do everything they can to protect you from danger. It doesn't matter if the means are rational or not; your parents feel the threat of AIDS intensely and are unlikely to change their minds easily. It doesn't mean they have no sympathy for your friend. It means they love you.

You might have to accept their fears and spend some time with this student while you're at school (adding in, when possible, a quick soda afterward). As time passes you might also try regularly showing your parents pamphlets or medical findings that clearly describe how one can and cannot contract AIDS.

Also, since your friend will undoubtedly sense your reluctance to pal around, gently let him know the fears are your parents' and not your own. It won't make him feel great, but it will help him feel less rejected by you.

HIV positive, he may not know it because he may have few or no symptoms. (AIDS is diagnosed when a person who is HIV positive begins to experience a particular set of symptoms.)

Drugs, of course, are horrible for you. They can ruin your health, mess up your mind, and kill you. These are reasons enough not to take them. But AIDS can also be passed by people who are high on drugs, not thinking straight, and therefore not protecting themselves and their partners from harm. Intravenous drug users are particularly vulnerable to the disease, as it can be transmitted through sharing contaminated needles.

There is no scientific evidence that AIDS can be passed in the saliva, but if you are concerned about kissing, talk to your doctor for his advice. It would be smart to avoid sharing food. This is true for any contagious disease (even the flu!). And whatever you do, don't engage in any "blood brother" activities in which you exchange blood to prove your allegiance to a buddy.

It's smart to concern yourself with AIDS. It's even smart to fear it. But it's not smart to behave as if you can get it anytime, anywhere, no matter what you do. And it's not fair or kind or smart to treat those people who have AIDS or are HIV positive as if they are nothing but a threat to you.

People who have AIDS are only a threat if they behave irresponsibly and you behave recklessly. Otherwise, people with AIDS are people in need of your support and companionship. They have far more to fear from you, in fact, than you do from them.

They are afraid you will walk away. Or reject them. Or leave them friendless. And on top of all there is to fear from AIDS itself, that would simply be too much.

You can stay safe without knowing who has AIDS. But if you do find out which student is sick, you should remember that kindness and companionship will not place you at any risk.

And if you happen to be the student who has AIDS, do seek out through your doctor a support group for other kids who carry the disease. Hopefully, should your friends find out you're sick, they will be understanding and supportive. But there are some painful things in life that only other people who share the misfortune can truly understand. They can offer the special kind of knowing help that you undoubtedly need.

Drinking problems

Q A few of your friends have been getting into drinking before, during, and after school. They're even starting to talk tough, as if they're looking for trouble. They keep insisting that you drink, too, but you don't want to. On the other hand, you don't want to lose your friends.

A It's a real drag when people you care about ask you to do things you just don't want to do or think are wrong. It makes no difference if the issue is drugs, alcohol, or cigarettes. It's scary. What if they stop liking you? What if you have to make a whole new set of friends? What if they start circulating rumors that you're weird, or uncool, or boring?

But here's the thing. What if you get hurt? What if doing something that is unlawful or unhealthy gets you into trouble and hurts others? And what if you begin to feel that only by doing exactly what your friends want will you have friends at all?

How will all of that feel?

In the situation described above, you first have to decide for yourself how you would define *friend*. Most people would agree a friend is someone with whom you can enjoy yourself. He is someone who understands you and whom you can understand, and someone who accepts you for what you are, though he may not like everything that is. Most of all, a friend is someone who cares about your well-being.

Next you need to understand something about cliques or gangs (which typically are rougher versions of cliques but which still come to life in similar ways). It is extremely difficult to go up against their power. That's how gangs get started. The kids don't all start feeling tough at the same time. They egg each other on. They pull it out of each other. Sometimes they even demand it, mostly from people who are just a little too insecure to stand up for what they might believe is a better way. "Okay. Let's do it," is easier to say than, "You know, I'm not sure I like this."

Then you need to consider exactly what you would be losing by standing up for what you believe. If you think friends are people who care about you, why would they want you to drink illegally? Why would they want you to plan or start a brawl at the local hangout? Why would that be a test of friendship? It makes no sense. If a friendship is based on really caring for each other, why is the test something that places everyone in a dangerous position?

Fighting with people for thrills is an angry, fruitless, and mean-spirited activity. Drinking is against the law, you will not be in full control of yourself, and if you don't directly get hurt as a result, indirect negative effects are bound to add up. Other friends will see that you're acting strange, your grades will slip, and you're liable to behave in irresponsible ways in many parts of your life.

Yet this is what your friends would have you do?

If you consider yourself a good friend of theirs, then give the relationship the respect it and you deserve by being honest and firm. You might fear that your friends would drop you, but that doesn't make it so. Sometimes our own feel-

HELP!

I saw this upperclassman trying to talk a kid in the grade below mine into taking drugs. It was disgusting. What should I do?

It's not a good idea to interfere during the conversation because you don't want to cause a direct conflict between yourself and the kid who is peddling drugs. As soon as possible, go straight to someone you trust at school (a favorite teacher or counselor) and tell him or her what you have witnessed.

As a result, the student who is selling drugs will be watched carefully, making it harder for him to approach younger, innocent kids. Don't wait for an arrest, however. That can't happen unless he's caught in the act of selling by a police officer.

ings of insecurity make us imagine other people are thinking the worst. We fear we're not cool, and so we think others know we're not cool. But that isn't the way things work. (Unless of course you slink around with your head down, as if no one would possibly be interested in you. Then you might have a public-image problem!)

Frankly state your position without being condescending or judgmental about your friends. Address how you feel about what they want you to do, taking care not to sound like some sort of know-it-all. "I'm sure I'll feel out of control, and I don't want that" or "I don't want to do something that's against the law. Aren't you guys nervous about that?" or "Drinking is just not my thing. It'll screw me up in school, and I don't want to do it. Period."

You might be surprised

by what happens. Sure, you may get teased or put down, but the truth is, if any one of these guys is your true friend, you will receive the respect you deserve. You might even give a few of them the strength to sit up and say, "Actually, I've been worrying about the same stuff." Maybe not at the moment that you say no. But possibly later.

And if you don't say no, and if these guys continue to harass you or actually reject your company, you'll have to be strong.

It's not easy standing up to a crowd, especially one you've depended on. But you don't have much choice.

As much as you've liked them and might still want to be with them, hopefully you like yourself more.

And that self will find new friends. People who like themselves always do.

Chapter 10

Who can help?

Hopefully, most of the time, things will go well for you. You'll have the usual ups and downs, with some situations being a little more upsetting than others. However, there should be nothing that you can't handle with the help of a good friend, a supportive parent, or just some quiet time on your own.

But on occasion even the most confident student will feel weighted down by a serious problem. It could easily happen to you. Your first reaction might be to handle it on your own. After all, doing so can make a person feel strong, capable, and mature.

But sometimes doing so isn't smart. In fact, often the strong, capable, mature thing to do is ask for help. This isn't easy. It can even be frightening. What if someone takes your problem too lightly? What if you choose the wrong person? What if this person doesn't understand? Or feels annoyed? Or thinks you're bad or dumb? What if what you confide in private gets spilled to other people? Worst of all, what if this person doesn't want to listen?

It might seem easier to just hide your troubles or share them with a good friend. But as wise as your friends may be, they may not have the mature insights you need to cope with your problem.

It's important to know that while school is primarily a place to concentrate on academics, it is also a place where many people are ready and able to help you with other, more personal concerns. There are certain professionals at your school who are there to offer you a perspective, a solution, or just simple understanding and support that kids your age simply cannot offer.

If you need help, give them a chance.

Who really cares?

Most of the adults in your school recognize that school-

work is not the only thing in your life. They know that personal problems can impact on your work. In fact, to greater or lesser degrees, many adults in your school hope to teach you more than just what is in your books. They want to help you think for yourself, mature, and cope with life.

People who go into education usually do so because they like working with children and teenagers. Certainly your teacher's primary concern is your schoolwork, but other professionals (and even some teachers) at your school are there to help you deal with painful family problems, friendship issues, and all the fears and anxieties you may occasionally have about yourself.

What does everyone do, anyway?

Each adult at school, however, does have a particular job. This doesn't mean you can't choose to speak to any one of them about a problem.

But each has a specific responsibility or area in which he or she is supposed to concentrate.

Not every school has on the premises, every day, each of these professionals. Still, in terms of the ones who are likely to be available to you, here are the basics of what they do.

Social workers or guidance counselors

These people are at school to help you with your academic program and/or any number of personal or family issues. They are there to discuss specific classroom concerns (for instance, if you're falling behind or not getting along with a teacher) as well as to help you establish better study habits. If you have a family problem, they are there to listen to the stress you might be feeling as well as to make some suggestions for dealing more effectively with a difficult parent or sibling relationship.

Social workers or guid-

ance counselors might schedule some regular counseling sessions with you so that you have someone to talk with during troubling times. They might also put together groups of students for a kind of support group to discuss painful or difficult topics.

You can elect to bring your parents into a meeting with either the social worker or the guidance counselor in order to help resolve difficult issues. If you are feeling, however, unusually unhappy or troubled, he or she might refer you to a school psychologist.

School psychologists

You may not have a psychologist at your school every day. He or she may only come in a few days a week, or may simply be "on call," meaning he or she comes in when needed.

Psychologists are trained to do a number of things within the school system. They can conduct individual or group counseling sessions with students. They are also specially trained to administer certain kinds of assessment tests to try and understand your behavior and feelings.

Here again, you can elect

H E L P !

I've been talking to this teacher that I like a lot about my problems with my mother, but the truth is, she's making me feel worse—guilty even!

People mean well. Sometimes they want to help so badly they forget to consider whether or not they're the best person for the job. If you are having some upsetting and personal conflicts with your mother, you may need to talk with someone who is trained to help you see the deeper issues in your relationship that could be causing the problems. A teacher may only be able to listen sympathetically to a surface problem. If you say, "My mother gets furious when I don't get A's!," she may respond gently by saying, "Well, she just knows how smart you are," which of course won't help. But a counselor might be able to uncover what's really upsetting you such as, "I never feel good enough," which, when discussed openly during a three-way conversation with your mother, might ease the problem.

In other words, not everyone who wants to help is always helpful! You have to go with your gut. If a person you have sought out is making you feel worse, something's wrong.

Try someone else.

to bring your parents into school to speak with the psychologist in order for your family members to gain a better understanding of one another. The school psychologist will look at how your particular family problems are affecting how you feel about yourself and your work. If, however, he or she thinks there is an important issue that needs to be worked out within the family (such as alcoholism or abuse, no matter how mild), or if for instance there is an angry divorce going on, he or she may recommend that all of

HELP!

I tried to talk to the school counselor about the problems I have getting along with other kids. But I felt like all she wanted to do was tell me what I did wrong.

First of all, tell her that's how you feel. She may be focusing too heavily on your role in the problem without acknowledging how the other kids are hurting you. By telling her how you feel, you'll be expressing what you need. You don't want to feel like the "bad guy." Hopefully she will reassure you.

And then she'll get back to what you were discussing. And here's why.

You know that your friends are being hurtful. She knows that, too. What's the point of discussing only that? Where will that get you? Sometimes, when we've having problems with friends, it's easier to think, "What's wrong with them?" rather than "What am I doing to make things

you see a family therapist outside of the school.

What are counseling sessions like?

At this point you are probably wondering what these counseling sessions are

worse?" Your counselor may simply be trying to get you to see that you aren't helping matters— that in some way you are participating in the problem. She may feel that the faster you own up to your contribution to the difficulty, the faster it will go away.

Of course, this isn't an easy thing to do.

No one likes admitting they've been making mistakes. But if you want to resolve a problem with other people, sometimes you have to look at yourself first.

all about. You may think it would be hard to trust people you barely know with your troubles. In fact, you may feel it's difficult to simply think about, much less talk about, all the issues that are on your mind. Shoving all those painful thoughts and feelings away may seem easier.

But understand that talking is very important. In fact, it's really your ticket to relief.

Through the act of talking with someone, you can bring your fears and anxieties out into the light. Hidden away, they can grow and fester. Talking about the fears openly, however, is the first step toward diminishing their power. Talk offers the opportunity to see yourself and your problems in a new, more constructive way. For instance, suppose you feel unlikable. You may discover you attract lots of people, but that you have a nasty habit of choosing on-again, off-again friends!

Counseling sessions are an opportunity to discuss *you* quietly and in private. No one will force you to talk about anything you'd rather not reveal. But you may find that after a few sessions you will want to confide even your deepest secrets, and that doing so feels good.

Counseling sessions are an opportunity to sit down with a person who wants to help you

HELP!

I let it slip to my parents that I've been speaking to the psychologist at school about stuff that's bothering me. They're furious!

Actually, they're probably not nearly as furious as they are threatened. They may feel like failures because you won't confide in them. They may fear they've done something terribly wrong and that you and the psychologist are tearing them apart. They may say you should handle your problems on your own like they do, because for them the idea of opening up to someone is terrifying or a sign of weakness.

But whatever they say, that psychologist is at your school for exactly the reason that you've been speaking with her. It is your right to take advantage of her skills so that you can feel better.

If your parents are making it very difficult for you, you might try telling them, right up front, that you know they love you and that it isn't their fault that you want to talk with this person. You just need to discuss things with someone who isn't so personally involved with you. Also, tell the psychologist about your parents' reaction and see what

be constructive and happy in your life. He or she will want to discuss anything that will help get you there. No problem is too small, and no problem is too big. These counselors have heard them all. You may fear they will laugh at the seeming insignificance of a problem (a friend has told you she doesn't like you anymore) or be horrified at the extent of a problem (you were sexually abused by a relative), but you will be wrong. The social worker or guidance counselor or psychologist may laugh, but only *with* you, as the two of you begin to discuss your worth, with or without the friend. And the counselor or psychologist may be horrified over the abuse, but only for the pain it's caused you. Not because they can't handle the difficulty or because you've revealed that a relative is disturbed.

she would suggest you say to soothe their anxieties.

If this doesn't work, suggest that your parents speak to the psychologist themselves so that they can better understand what happens during your sessions. (The psychologist will not reveal anything private you have shared with her when she meets with them.)

Again, remember that your parents are not nearly as mad as they are scared. They don't want to feel bad or blamed or inadequate.

But the important thing to remember is, neither do you.

Teachers

Your teacher's primary responsibility is to teach the material you must cover in a given year. But most teachers also believe they are there to teach things about life. This would include responsibility, honesty, helpfulness, sociability, and more. The classroom offers an opportunity for students to work together, and in so doing it becomes a terrific laboratory for guiding you toward socially responsible behavior.

Some teachers also take a very keen personal interest in their students. Certainly there are those who are burned out. They have been at the profession a long time and are somewhat tired of or disinterested in anything but their specific academic responsibilities. But there are still those teachers who are very aware of and

---

HELP!

But I'm often so bored at school! Why do I have to learn all this stuff?

Though you're probably tired of hearing it, you need school. You have a long life ahead of you, and there's a lot to know so that you can lead it productively. Sometimes what you're learning at school won't seem relevant. Worse, it will feel like a useless bore. After all, what does knowing the names of the planets have to do with, say, becoming a nurse? Why memorize the famous speech from *Julius Caesar* if you want to become an engineer?

These are fair questions. Here's the answer.

Knowing the planets or Shakespeare *won't* help you become a nurse or engineer. But it may help you do a better job, relate to others, and feel good about yourself. Being a well-rounded person is an extremely useful quality. Let's look ahead for a minute. Suppose you have a sick patient who is into astronomy. What if she wants you to sit and talk a while? Imagine how nice it would be for her to converse

concerned with the well-being of their students and are more than happy to talk privately about issues that may be disturbing them.

You should not try to talk to a teacher directly before or after a class; instead, make an appointment with the teacher so that the two of you can talk quietly and alone.

The principal

The school principal has a very big job that touches just about everything in the school. He (or she) is as concerned about the school's re-

with someone who knows something about it. Or suppose you're an engineer applying for a job and the potential employer is concerned. He has a small company, lots of clients, and wants whomever he employs to be able to relate to all sorts of people, not just other engineers. During the course of a discussion, you humorously quote Shakespeare to make a point. He will be extremely impressed. He will also think you and his varied clients will get on just fine.

It's important to know things. You may not see it now, but you will later. You're probably tired of hearing that, but being tired of it doesn't mean it's wrong.

It just means you may not really get it yet.

That's okay. You won't fully until you're in a position to be glad about what you know.

You're living in the present now, but you have a future self.

Keep him or her in mind as you go through school.

He or she needs to know a lot . . . and he or she needs your help.

Bored or not.

cycling program, teachers' salaries, and the electric bill as he is about the teachers themselves and the general well-being of the student body.

Truthfully, the principal is usually considered the last stop for a classroom problem or even a very troubled student. Teachers, counselors, and psychologists will usually try and work out the difficulty with a student before they consider bringing the issue to the principal.

This does not mean that the principal isn't interested in you. But his job is manifold and he simply cannot take on every difficulty every student encounters. Some principals, in fact, are particularly sorry about that and try and make themselves, when they can, accessible. You can tell if you have one of those! He is usually found walking through the halls, stopping to chat with various students. He may pop into classrooms just to see how things are

going, and actually invite students in at various times to talk over anything that's bothering them about school.

Not all principals are open for this kind of dialogue, because the demands of their particular school simply do not allow for this kind of regular interaction.

Which brings us to perhaps the most important issue.

With all these people around, how do you know the right person to speak to?

There is no right person. What matters most is whether or not you feel a connection with the person in whom you decide to confide. You may not know this in advance. You may start talking to one person, discover you don't feel comfortable with her or him, and opt to continue the talk with someone else. On the other hand, you may already sense that a

GUIDANCE OFFICE

particular person is right. Perhaps it's a teacher with whom you have a great relationship. It might be a guidance counselor who has spoken to your class about drug use, or some other issue, who seems a terrific, open person.

You have to go with your gut. And you also have to allow this person to let you know if you need to speak with someone who has more knowledge or better skills in dealing with a particular problem. You should not take this as a rejection. A teacher may not feel equipped to help you build your self-confidence if it is sagging perilously low. A social worker may think you need to speak to a psychologist if you are living with a troubled parent who is making you miserable.

And don't be afraid to look everywhere in the school to begin the process of opening up. A particular baseball coach may have struck you as someone who would understand. Or perhaps the art teacher, who likely has

nothing at all to do with the problem you are having with your algebra teacher, could help!

The most important thing to do is *ask for help if you need it.* Don't worry about going to the exact right person. You will get there one way or another. What you need to do most of all is start talking.

A note about privacy

You are entitled to privacy. You have the right to assume that what you choose to share with a counselor is between the two of you. If the problem you are discussing might be eased by the introduction of another person into the talks, that is for you and your counselor to decide together. Your counselor should not bring in a parent, teacher, or friend without your agreement. The exception to this rule is if your counselor believes you or someone you are talking about is in physical danger. If you were contemplating hurting yourself in some way, or if you reported that someone was threatening you or herself, your counselor would feel compelled to do something about it.

Other than this kind of dire circumstance, what you say in private should remain private. That is both an unspoken and spoken agreement between counselor and student and you should be able to rely upon it. However, if you feel better making sure,

simply tell the counselor, "I need to know this is just between us." He will assure you of your right to privacy.

So if you're feeling overwhelmed by a problem, whether it's academic or personal, check out which people at your school have the job of listening. See who you feel comfortable with, and then start talking.

It's the best way to start feeling better.

The payback

There are a lot of "have-to's" related to school. You have to go. You have to do your homework. You have to study. You have to be polite to the teachers. You have to participate.

The list is endless.

But even despite all those have-to's, one thing remains absolutely true.

The kind of education you get is up to you.

No one can make you stick up for your rights, concentrate, do the best you can, or get the most out of all the classes you have to take.

No one can make you care.

You either will or you won't, or somewhere in between. But however you opt to be involved in the school experience, it's you who will live with the outcome. If you put your all into it, you'll get a lot back. If you don't, you won't.

Amazingly, despite all of the rules, all of the expectations, all of the pressures, what happens in school is very much up to you.

INDEX

A

Abuse, 170-74
  of friend, 170-74
  talking to school profes-
    sional about, 171-74, 254
Accusations:
  of being bossy, 217-19
  by student trying to pick
    fight, 233
  wrongful, of cheating, 90-93
  wrongful, of whispering in
    class, 27
Acting, casting
  decisions and, 213-16
Advanced classes:
  being moved to, 107-10
  catching up in, 109
After-school hours:
  schedule for, 125
  see also Extracurricular
    activities; Sports
Age differences:
  acting cool and, 69
  feeling awkward due to, 68-70
AIDS (autoimmune deficiency
    syndrome), 227-28, 241-45
  HIV transmission and, 241-
    43, 244

  privacy rights and, 241-42
  showing kindness to people
    with, 244-45
Alcoholism, 254
Anxiety:
  challenges and, 108-10
  deep-breathing and, 119
  public speaking and, 133-35
  talking about, 255
  test taking and, 116-20
  visualization and, 119, 134-35
Apologizing, 55
Athletes, professional,
  192-93
Athletics. See Sports
Attitude, "fitting in" and, 52-53
Attractiveness, worries about, 62-63
Awkwardness, feelings of, 68-70

B

Back-biting, 57
Bad influences:
  grades and, 152, 153
  parental views on, 151-55
  reality tests and, 151-52
Baseball:
  bench warming in, 181-84
  see also Sports

Basketball:
  endless drills in, 178-80
  expectations of spectators
    and teammates in, 187-89
  see also Sports
Bathrooms, concern for physical
  safety in, 232
Bench warming, 181-84
"Blood brother" activities, 244
Boasting, by violent students,
  240
Body, self-consciousness about,
  70-72
Book reports:
  turned in late, 143-46
  unfair grade on, 102-4
Boredom, at school, 258-59
Bossiness:
  of committee chairpeople,
    217-19
  of project partners, 141-42
Boyfriends and girlfriends:
  ex-, dealing with, 73-74
  no luck with, 61-63
"Brown-nosing," 19-20, 21
Buses, fears for physical
  safety on, 229-31
"Buttering up" teachers, 19-20, 21

C

Careless teachers, 31-33
Casting, of school plays, 213-16
Catching up:
  after being moved to advanced
    class, 109
  on missed homework
    assignments, 130-31
Challenges, rising to, 108-10

Changes:
  coping with, 14
  favorite teacher's departure
    and, 14-16
  feeling awkward due to, 68-70
Cheating, 79-98

  alternatives to, 83-84
  "changing" your report card
    and, 96-98
  consequences of, 81-82, 87-89
  friend's request to copy and,
    82-85
  getting caught at, 85, 86-89
  homework copying and, 84
  inadvertent plagiarism and,
    93-95
  paper copying and, 88
  protesting to fellow student
    about, 92
  reasons for, 80-81, 87
  on tests, 82-85, 87, 90-93
  wrongful accusations of, 90-93
Chores, tough homework
  assignments and, 146
Class assignments, friends
  separated by, 49-51

Classes:
  advanced, 107-10
  asking questions in, 11-13
  slow, 105-7
  whispering in, 27, 30
Class president, competing with
    friend for, 58-60
Cliques, 246
  see also Crowds
Clothes, 51-53
  "fitting in" and, 52-53
Coaches, 190
  endless drills of, 178-80
  expectations of, 177
  players left on bench by, 181-84
  pressure of, 188
College, grades and, 191
Committees:
  bossy chairpeople of, 217-19
  delegating power in, 218-19
  dropping out of, 223
Comparisons:
  to academically successful
    sibling, 161-66
  to athletically successful
    sibling, 197
  danger of, 166
Competition:
  with friend, 58-60, 118
  for job on school paper,
    209-12
  with sibling, 163
Conflicts:
  with friends, 42, 43, 44
  with parents, 253
Congratulations, offering of,
    60, 182
"Cool":
  drinking and, 246, 247-48

"uncool" extracurricular
    activities and, 207-9
  violent behavior and, 240
  wanting to be, 69
Copying:
  friend's request and, 82-85
  from homework, 84
  inadvertent plagiarism and,
    93-95
  of report or paper, 88
  from test paper, 82-85, 87,
    90-93
Counseling sessions, 255-56
Counselors. See Guidance
    counselors; Psychologists
Cramming, 117
Criticism, public humiliation
    and, 29-31
Crowds:
  changes in dynamics of, 220
  downsides of being in, 56
  importance of belonging to,
    208
  interests not shared by, 207-9
  rejection by, 54-58
  rumors in, 55
  stepping away from, 56, 58
  wild, joined by friend, 64-67
  wild, parental disapproval
    of, 151-55
  wild, parting from, 75-77
Crushes, on teachers, 34-36
"Curve," scoring tests on, 112

D

Death, of family member, 168
Debate team, cool crowd's
    disdain for, 207-9

Deep-breathing, before tests, 119
Delegating power, in committees, 218-19
Denial, bad grades and, 165
Depression, 125
  of friend, 67
Difficult tests, 111-12
Disappointment, dealing with, 182-83, 186, 213-16
Discipline, in sports, 176-77, 180
Dislike:
  explanations for, 26-27
  of teacher for student, 24-28
Disobedience, sneaking around and, 154
Divorce, 168, 254-55
Drills, in sports:
  endless, 178-80
  purpose of, 179-80
Drinking problems, 245-48
Drugs:
  AIDS and, 242, 244
  friend's experimentation with, 64
  peddled by upperclassmen, 247

E

Embarrassment:
  about average grades, 44-46
  about body, 70-72
  about great grades, 121-22
Essay writing, 113-15
  importance of writing skills and, 113, 115
  structuring ideas in, 114-15
Ex-boyfriends or -girlfriends, dealing with, 73-74
Excuses:

for bad report card, 158
for undone homework, 129
Expectations:
  of coaches, 177
  for extracurricular activities, 201
  of parents, 148-50, 159-61
  of spectators and teammates at sports events, 187-89
Extracurricular activities, 199-224
  bossy committee chairpeople in, 217-19
  casting decisions and, 213-16
  dropping out of, 222-24
  and interests not shared by crowd, 207-9
  job jealousy in, 209-12
  non-macho interests and, 202-6
  purpose of, 200-201, 207-8
  time for friends curtailed by, 201, 219-22
  tough homework assignments and, 146
  see also Sports

F

Family, 147-74
  abusive behavior in, 170-74, 254
  major problems in, 131, 167-74, 254-55
  see also Parents; Siblings
Family therapy, 254-55
Favoritism, teacher's pets and, 17-21
Fears:
  of public speaking, 133-34
  talking about, 255

see also Physical fears
Femininity, 203
    athletic abilities and, 195
Fights, 246
    on school buses, 229-31
    student's attempt to start, 233
Financial problems, 168
"Fitting in," 52-53, 122
    special abilities and, 204-5
Football:
    not making team in, 182-83
    see also Sports
Footnotes, 95
Forgery, of parent's signature
    on report card, 96-98
French club, disappointment
    with, 222-24
Friends, 41-77
    abused at home, 170-74
    anxiety level among, before
        tests, 119-20
    balancing other responsibilities
        with, 44
    campaigning for class office
        against, 58-60
    caring for, 64-67
    casting decisions and, 214-15
    cheating by, 82-85
    choice of, 49
    competition with, 58-60, 118
    definition of, 246
    with drinking problems,
        245-48
    feeling uncomfortable with,
        75-77
    financial disparities and, 51-53
    grades compared by, 44-46
    with greater athletic successes,
        182-83

handling great grades with,
    121-22
hiding things from, 122
mixed feelings about, 42-43
new, 56

parental disapproval of, 151-55
problems getting along with,
    254-55
as project partners, 140-41
rejection by, 54-58
responding to attack on,
    234-36
saying mean things behind
    one's back, 57
separated by class assignments,
    49-51
sharing problems with,168-69,
    173, 251
teacher's preference for, 19
teasing by, 47-48, 61-63, 122,
    202-3
time for, curtailed by
    extracurricular activities,
    201, 219-22
upsetting problems with,
    128-32
wild crowd joined by, 64-67
see also Boyfriends and
    girlfriends

G

Gangs, 246
  see also Crowds
Gay teachers, 38
Gender roles, 203
  nonmacho interests and, 202-6
  sports and, 195
Generosity, allowing friend to
  copy confused with, 85
Girlfriends. See Boyfriends
  and girlfriends
Girls, athletic, masculinity
  ascribed to, 195
Grades, 99-122
  bad, facing parents with,
    156-58
  bad influence of friends and,
    152, 153
  "changing," on report card,
    96-98
  compared by friends, 44-46
  consequences of, 149
  on difficult tests, 112
  drinking and, 247
  feeling embarrassed about,
    44-46
  good, being moved to
    advanced class and, 107,
    109-10
  great, handling of, 121-22
  "magical" powers and messages
    attached to, 100-101
  parental expectations and,
    159-61
  poor, being moved to slow
    class and, 105-7
  poor, denial and, 165
  poor, meaning of, 117-19

problems at home and, 167-69
  purpose of, 100
  question asking and, 11, 13
  sibling comparisons and, 162
  slipping, sports and, 189-93
  tutoring and, 47
  unfair, 26, 102-4
Growing pains, 69
Guidance counselors, 5, 132,
    169, 252, 260
  abuse at home and, 171-74
  counseling sessions with, 255-57
Gym:
  self-consciousness in locker
    room and, 70-72
  showering after, 72
  see also Sports

H

Hallways, hassles in, 231-33
Harassment, sexual, 36-40
Heartbreak, 73-74
Help:
  on homework, 126-28
  running for, 234-36
Heroics, running for help vs.,
    234-36
HIV (human immunodeficiency
    virus), 228, 243-44
  transmission of, 241-43, 244
Home. See Family; Parents;
  Siblings
Homework, 123-46
  after-school schedule and, 125
  bossy project partners and,
    141-42
  catching up on missed
    assignments and, 130-31

friend's desire to copy from, 84
help at home on, 126-28
irresponsible project partners and, 139-42
late assignments and, 143-46
lazy project partners and, 136-39
oral reports and, 133-35
overly heavy load of, 144
planning ahead and, 144-46
purpose of, 125
undone, 125, 128-32
Homosexuality, 206
of teachers, 38
Humiliation, in front of class, 29-31

I

Image, student government and, 210-11
Independence, desire for,153-55

K, L

Kissing, AIDS and, 244
Late homework assignments, 143-46
Lazy project partners, 136-39
Lead sentences, in essays, 114-15
Listening, to advice, 155

Locker room, self-consciousness in, 70-72
Loneliness, problems at home and, 167, 168

M

Masculinity, 203
non-macho interests and, 202-6
sports and, 195
Math:
being moved to advanced class in, 109
difficult tests in, 111-12
Mistakes, admitting to, 86-87, 254-55
Money:
financial problems at home and, 168
inequalities in, 51-53
Motivation, 150
knowing what you want and, 189
parents' attempts at, 163
Music:
special abilities in, 204-5
time for friends curtailed by, 219-22

N

Name-calling, "teacher's pet" and, 17-21
Newspaper, competition for jobs on, 209-12
New students, 52
Nonmacho interests, 202-6
Notes, for oral reports, 135

O

Oral reports, 133-35
  notes for, 135
Orchestra, special musical
  abilities and, 204-5

P

Papers:
  copying of, 88
  inadvertent plagiarism in,
    93-95
Parents, 43
  abusive, 170-74, 254
  AIDS threat and, 243
  conflicts with, 253
  disapproving of your friends,
    151-55
  disobedience to, 154
  divorce of, 168, 254-55
  expectations of, 148-50,
    159-61
  fighting of, 167-69
  help on homework from, 126-
    28
  inattentive, 150
  professionals at school and,
    252, 254, 256-57
  report cards and, 96-98,
    156-58
  siblings compared by, 161-66
  teachers' conferences with,
    26, 28, 32, 98
  tough homework assignments
    and, 146
  volunteering at school
    events, 157
Partners, for projects:

bossy, 141-42
friends as, 140-41
irresponsible, 139-42
lazy, 136-39

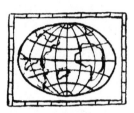

Perfectionism, parental
  expectations and, 159-61
Performance anxiety, 108-10
  oral reports and, 133-35
  test taking and, 116-20
Physical advances, of teachers,
  36-40
Physical fears, 225-48
  AIDS and, 227-28, 241-45
  drinking problems and, 245-
    48
  drug peddling at school and,
    247
  hallway hassles and, 231-33
  reporting other students'
    plans and, 237-38
  running for help and, 234-36
  witnessing attack and,
    239-41
Plagiarism, inadvertent, 93-95
Planning ahead:
  after-school schedule and,
    125
  for long-term assignments,
    144-46
Plays, casting of, 213-16
Play time, scheduling of, 125

Poetry club, teasing of boys
    in, 202-6
Politics:
    image vs. issues in, 210-11
    see also Student government
"Potential," not working to,
    21-23
Power, bossiness and, 217-19
Practice, in sports, 176-77,
    190
    endless drills in, 178-80
Pressure:
    of living up to successful
        sibling, 161-66, 197
    parental expectations and,
        148-50, 159-61
    put on oneself, 162
    in sports, 177, 184-86, 188,
        197
Principals, 5, 259-60
    safety issues and, 230, 232
Privacy:
    counseling by professionals
        at school and, 261-62
    problems at home or with
        friends and, 131-32
    sick student's right to,
        241-42
Problems:
    at home, 131, 167-74, 254
    leaving behind, 167-68

school professionals to onsult
    about, 5, 249-62
    sharing with others, 168-69,
        173, 251
Professional athletics, 192-93
Professionals, at school, 5,
    249-62
    abuse and, 170-74, 254-55
    choosing among, 260-61
    counseling sessions with,
        255-57
    privacy rights and, 261-62
    see also Guidance
        counselors; Principals;
        Psychologists; Social
        workers
Project partners. *See* Partners, for
    projects
Psychologists, 5, 132, 252-57,
    260
    abuse at home and, 171-74
    counseling sessions with,
        255-57
    functions of, 252-53
    privacy rights and, 261-62
Public speaking:
    fear of, 133-34
    preparing for, 134-35
Punishment, for cheating,
    87-89

Q

Questions:
    about grades, 44-46
    reluctance to ask, 11-13
    teacher annoyed at, 12
Quizzes, surprise, 131

R

Reading assignments, falling behind in, 130-31
Reality tests:
 for bad influence of friends, 151-52
 for sensation of being disliked by teacher, 24-25
Rebelling, 153
 against high-pressure parents, 160-61
Rejection, by friends, 54-58
Remembering, personal prompters and, 114
Report cards:
 bad, facing parents with, 156-58
 "changing" grades in, 96-98
 facing up to bad grades in, 165

Reports:
 copying of, 88
 oral, 133-35
 partners for. See Partners, for projects
 research, inadvertent plagiarism in, 93-95
 turned in late, 143-46
 unfair grades on, 102-4

Research papers, inadvertent plagiarism in, 93-95
Research papers, inadvertant plagiarism in, 93-95
Respect, 9
Romance. See Boyfriends and girlfriends
Rudeness, 30
Rumors, 55, 57, 245-46
Running for help, 234-36

S

Safety issues. See Physical fears
Schedule:
 for after-school hours, 125
 for long-term assignments, 144-46
School buses, fears for physical safety on, 229-31
Secrecy, 122
 see also Privacy
Self-confidence, 196
 poor grades and, 105-6, 191
Self-consciousness:
 in front of upperclassmen, 68-70
 in locker room, 70-72
Self-discipline, 98
Sexual harassment, 36-40
Sexual intercourse, AIDS and, 242
Sexually transmitted diseases, 227-28, 241-45
 see also AIDS
Sexual orientation:
 development of, 206
 of teachers, 38
 teasing about, 202-6

Showering, after gym, 72
Siblings, 43
    academic successes of, 161-66
    athletic successes of, 197
    comparisons to, 30, 161-66,
        197
    competition between, 163
    help on homework from, 127
Sickness, of family member, 168
Signature, forgery of, 96-98
Sloppily written work, 29-30
Slow classes, being moved to,
        105-7
Sneaking around, 154
Social life:
    parental presure and, 159,
        160, 161
    see also Boyfriends and
    girlfriends; Crowds; Friends
Social workers, 5, 252, 260
    counseling sessions with,
        255-57
Softball:
    teammates' pressure in,
        184-86
    see also Sports
Spectators, at sports events,
        187-88
Sports, 175-90
    achieving balance between
        academics and, 190
    alternative, 198
    attraction of, 194-95
    bench warming in, 181-84
    deciding whether to
        participate in, 177, 180,
        183-84, 190-93
    discipline needed in, 176-77,
        180

endless drills in, 178-80
lack of athletic abilities and,
    194-98
not making team in, 182-83
practice in, 176-80, 190
pressure in, 177, 184-86, 188
professional athletics and,
    192-93
sibling comparisons and, 197
slipping grades and, 189-93
spectators' and teammates'
    expectations and, 187-89
teamwork in, 177
tough homework assignments
    and, 146
Staring, accusations of, 233
Student government:
    competing with friend for
        office in, 58-60
    image vs. issues and, 210-11
Students:
    abused, 170-74, 254
    AIDS-afflicted, 241-45
    cheating by, 79-98;
        see also Cheating
    consumer rights of, 31-33
    crushes of, 34-36
    disliked by teacher, 24-28
    extracurricular activities
        of, 199-224; see also
        Extracurricular activities;
        Sports
    family life of, 147-74; see
        also Family; Parents;
        Siblings
    grades of, 99-122; see also
        Grades
    hassled in hallways, 231-33
    homework of, 123-46; see

also Homework
mutual respect between
  teachers and, 9
new to class, 52
physical fears of, 225-48;
  see also Physical fears
picking fights on school
  buses, 229-31
"potential" of, 21-23
professional help available
  to, 5, 249-62
public humiliation of, 29-31
  reluctant to ask questions,
  11-13
self-conscious in locker
  room, 70-72
social life of, 41-77, 159,
  160, 161; *see also*
  Boyfriends and girlfriends;
  Crowds; Friends

teacher's inappropriate
  advances toward, 36-40
as teacher's pet, 17-21
under attack, getting help for,
  234-36
unfair accusations against, 27
witnessing violent acts of,
  239-41
Studying:
  catching up on missed
    assignments and, 130-31
  for tests, 117
Support groups, 252

T

Tattling:
  as helping, 67
  on students planning violent
    act, 237-38
  teacher's unfair questions
    and, 27
Teachers, 5, 7-40
  abuse at home and, 173-74
    after-school appointments
    with, 232
  asking questions of, 11-13
  bad influences as perceived
    by, 151, 153
  careless, 31-33
  contracts of, 33
  crushes on, 34-36
  favoritism of, 17-21
  feeling disliked by, 24-28
  gay, 38
  help at home and, 126-28
  lateness with assignments
    and, 145
  leaving in middle of school
    year, 14-16
  mutual respect between
    students and, 9
  parents' conferences with,
    26, 28, 32, 98
  playing up to, 18-20
  "potential" as perceived by,
    21-23
  problems with project partner-

ships and, 138-39, 142
siblings compared by, 30
students humiliated by, 29-31
students' personal problems and,
169, 251, 253, 257-59, 260
too-friendly, 36-40
undone homework and,
128-32
unfair accusations of, 27
unfair grades given by, 102-4
Teacher's pets, 17-21
Teammates:
expectations of, 188-89
pressure of, 184-86
Teamwork, 142
in extracurricular activities,
218-19
in sports, 177
see also Partners, for projects
Teasing:
about bad luck with opposite
sex, 61-63
about girl's athleticism, 195
about great grades, 122
about lack of athletic abilities,
196
in locker room or shower, 72
about mother attending school
events, 157
motivation for, 61-62
about nonmacho interests,
202-6
responses to, 63
about tutor, 47-48
Tennis, 185-86, 197
see also Sports
Tests:
cheating on, 82-85, 87, 90-93
consequences of doing poorly

on, 117-19
difficult, 111-12
essay writing on, 113-15
as measurement, 116-17
nervousness during, 116-20
remembering details on, 114
scored on "curve," 112

surprise quizzes and, 131
unfair, 81
visualization before, 119
Theater, casting decisions and,
213-16
Tutoring, 190
to compensate for careless
teacher, 33
help on homework in, 127
teasing about, 47-48
writing skills and, 114

U

Upperclassmen:
drug dealing by, 247
self-consciousness in front of,
68-70

V

Venting, 164
Victims, choosing of, 232-33

Violence, 227
    boasting about, 240
    choice of victims and, 232-33
    explanations for, 240
    hallway hassles and, 231-33

    heroics and, 234-36
    reporting other students'
        plans for, 237-38
    running for help and, 234-36

    on school buses, 229-31
    witnessing of, 239-41
Visualization:
    public speaking and, 134-35
    test taking and, 119
Volunteering:
    by parents, 157
    by students, 240

W

Whispering in class, 27, 30
Witnessing an attack, 239-41
Writing skills:
    essay writing and, 113-15
    need for, 113, 115